ANCIENT ROME 2nd Edition
STUDENT BOOK

Fran Rutherford

Illustrated by James Rutherford

Ancient Rome, Student Book
Second Edition, July 2011

Copyright ©2005 Fran Rutherford, Black Forest, Colorado
www.classicstudyguides.com

All Rights Reserved
For permission to use more than short excerpts for critical reviews, contact the author through Aquinas and More, 1331 Red Cedar Cr., Ft. Collins, CO 80524 / 800-428-2820

Trademark Notice
Questions for the Thinker™ is a trademark belonging to Fran Rutherford. Materials with this trademark have previously been published by Kolbe Academy and Mother's House Publishing. However, this version is a new, updated and more complete edition and the only one currently authorized. No duplication of content is permitted without written permission from the author.

Original illustrations, cover design and interior layout by James Rutherford, Colorado Springs, Colorado

Published by Aquinas and More
www.aquinasandmore.com
Fort Collins, Colorado

ISBN 978-0-9837581-8-1
Made in the United States of America

I dedicate this work to the following:

I dedicate this work to my parents, Luis and Agatha Gastellum.
Thank you for the many lessons you taught me. Among them:

- Love of God
- Love of Family
- Love of Country
- Love of Creation
- Love of Learning

I am grateful for the countless sacrifices you made so that we could all pursue our dreams. By your example, I learned that you are never too old to learn, nor are you too old to try something new if called to do so.

May you rest in peace.

Table of Contents

Why Study Ancient Rome?	I
Instructions for the Student and the Teacher	IV
Pronunciation Guide	V
Significant Dates in Ancient Rome	VI

Unit 1: Poetry — 1
THE AENEID — 3
Book I	5
Book II	6
Book III	7
Book IV	8
Book V	10
Book VI	11
Book VII	13
Book VIII	14
Book IX	15
Book X	16
Book XI	17
Book XII	18
Book I	22
Book II	23
Book III	25
Book IV	26
Book V	27
Book VI	28
Book VII	29
Book VIII	31
Book XI	32
Book XII	33
Book XIII	34
Book XIV	35
Book XV	36

Unit 2: History — 39
THE EARLY HISTORY OF ROME — 41
Book I	42
Book II	44
Book III	47
Book IV	50
Book V	51
Book XXI	56
Book XXII	57
Book XXIII	57
Book XXVI	58
Book XXVIII	59
Book XXIX	60
Book XXX	60

THE CONSPIRACY OF CATILINE — 63
Chapter 1	65
Chapter II	65
Chapter III	66
Chapter IV	67
Chapter V	67
Chapter VI	67
Chapter VII	68

About Cicero and His Work	70
ATTACK ON AN ENEMY OF FREEDOM	71
ATTACK ON MISGOVERNMENT	75

THE ANNALS OF IMPERIAL ROME — 77
Book I	78
Book II	80
Book III	82
Book IV	84
Book V	85
Book VI	85
Book XI	86
Book XII	87
Book XIII	88
Book XIV	88
Book XV	89
Book XVI	91

Unit 3: Drama — 93
Roman Drama	94

THE BROTHERS MENAECHMI	97
Prologue	98
Act I	98
Act II	98
Act III	99
Act IV	100
Act V	100
THE BROTHERS	103
Act I	104
Act II	104
Act III	104
Act IV	105
Act V	105

Unit IV: Philosophy ~ Religion

	107
MEDITATIONS	109
Book I	110
Book II	110
Book III	111
Book IV	111
Book V	112
Book VI	112
Book VII	113
Book VIII	113
Book IX	114
Book X	115
Book XI	115
Book XII	116
SELECTIONS FROM EARLY CHRISTIAN WRITINGS	119
Clement of Rome	120
Letter to the Ephesians	121
Letter to the Romans	122
The Martyrdom of Polycarp	123
The Didache	124
St. Augustine and His Works	126
THE CONFESSIONS: BOOKS I-X	129
Book I	130
Book II	131
Book III	131
Book IV	132
Book V	132
Book VI	133
Book VII	134
Book VIII	134
Book IX	135
Book X	135
THE CITY OF GOD: BOOKS I-X	137
Book I	138
Book II	139
Book III	140
Book IV	142
Book V	143
Book VI	145
Book VII	145
Book VIII	146
Book IX	147
Book X	148
Sources Consulted	151
About the Author	153
About the Illustrator	153

Why Study Ancient Rome?

To the modern mind, it may seem an esoteric exercise to read the literature and history of Ancient Rome. What can the Roman senators, stoic philosophers, corrupt emperors, overly ambitious conquerors and comedians possibly have to say to us in the 21st century? After all, didn't Rome fall? It must not have been worth saving if it suffered such a monumental decline.

We cannot understand ourselves or our modern institutions if we do not understand Rome. It was in the farming settlements of Italy that people came to value strength and self-discipline, as well as persistence, thrift, loyalty, industriousness and a sense of destiny. With those virtues firmly implanted in her heart, Rome grew to be the greatest empire the world had ever seen, and it was the stability of that empire that allowed for the tremendous growth of Roman influence and culture. For over a thousand years, Rome grew and civilized her neighbors and brought the barbarians into her sphere of influence.

We are left today with the physical remnants of Rome in the architecture which has endured. The Romans perfected the use of concrete, which enabled them to construct such massive works as the Coliseum and the Pantheon with its large dome. Outside of Italy, travelers to Spain, England, Africa and Asia can see the remains of aqueducts which brought life-saving water to the population centers and could thus promote a settled life and the growth of culture. Under Hadrian, a wall was built in Britain which was 73 miles long, had 14 forts and at mile-intervals had garrisons which could hold 100 men. The Roman roads united the empire and facilitated the exchange of ideas and goods among the people of Europe in ways which were never possible before. It was those roads which enabled the idea of Christianity to spread so rapidly throughout the empire, and eventually beyond it.

As permanent and notable as the physical remains of Rome are, more important are the institutions which were established to bring order to private and public life. The Roman family was of utmost importance and was subject to the *pater familias* (father of the family). One example of the importance of family was seen in people's names. Among the men, the middle name or *nomen*, referred to the clan from which a person came. The third name, or *cognomen*, referred to the particular branch of the clan one came from. The first name, or *praenomen*, identified the individual (Marcus Tullius Cicero). Women carried their identifying first name as well as their father's name and then a third name which indicated their birth rank among the girls of the family (*Maior, Secunda, etc*). Influences of this system are seen among many peoples today, even though the names may identify different relationships. Spanish men, for example, carry their first name, the surname of their father and then the maiden name of the mother (Luis Gastellum Acuña). Women in that society carry their family name as well as that of their husband, often, but not always, preceded by de, meaning of, or with the use of a hyphen (Agueda Cota de Gastellum or Águeda Gastellum-Cota). The use of a name followed by II or Jr. is common today and usually indicates that a son carries the exact name as his father.

It was not a huge leap from *pater familias* to the acceptance by the people of the authority of the State and then the emperor who was known as the *pater patriae* (father of the country). Rome used her army to build the empire, but she did not generally destroy the people she conquered. Rather, she established the rule of law in the provinces, she granted citizenship to the conquered provincials, she offered protection against barbarian invaders, she tolerated the differences in culture and religion, and she facilitated the exchange of goods and ideas. Following on the heels of her legions, Rome sent governors and government workers (the forerunners of our civil service workers), architects, merchants and craftsmen who created an extension of Rome wherever they went.

The importance of citizenship cannot be overlooked, because citizens of Rome had privileges and protections which others did not. In the *Acts of the Apostles* 25:13-21, the story is related

of the case against St. Paul being referred to King Agrippa. He was being held in custody in Caesarea, and the Jews were demanding his condemnation. Festus told the Jews that it was not the Roman way to hand an accused man over before he had a chance to defend himself and meet his accusers face-to-face. Paul appealed for an imperial judgment, and the local governor had no choice but to send him to Rome. The concept of the rule of law cannot and must not be underestimated. For the times it was a new concept, and it was extended throughout the empire. From Rome we inherited the idea that a man is innocent until proven guilty, an idea and practice which is at the foundation of our legal system today.

In the days of the empire there were three classes of free Romans. The upper class consisted of the patricians, those who held hereditary offices. Under that class were the equestrians, or knights. They were the business class. On the bottom were the plebians and freemen who composed the bulk of the population. The plebians gradually grew in power as their numbers increased, and this was reflected in the establishment of the tribunes to represent them in the government. This idea of representation is seen today in the British Parliament which consists of a House of Lords and a House of Commons. In the United States we have a Senate and a House of Representatives. The foundations of these institutions were laid in Ancient Rome. At the bottom of society were the slaves. They were taken from conquered people and were the labor force for massive Roman projects. Slaves didn't share in the benefits of Roman society. Though for the majority life was difficult, some distinguished themselves, rose to prominence and earned their freedom.

Rome had various forms of government. It went from a monarchy (rule by a king) to a republic (rule by two consuls with a senate and two assemblies) and finally to an empire (rule by an emperor). No single form was perfect, and certainly corruption existed at every level. But the greatness of Rome was that she established the rule of law, and during the time of the Republic, she laid out the plan for a government in which the people would have a part. There were always struggles for power between the classes, but the idea of the rule of law had been established, and it would endure through the centuries. The rule of law has not been successful in the parts of the world which have had no historical links to Rome.

Rome had looked to Greece for inspiration and took those inspirations and made them her own. While the Greeks enjoyed ethical discussion and sought to discover what constituted a life well-lived, the Romans relied more on their ancient traditions as their guide to behavior. While the Greeks sought to illustrate beauty and their view of the ideal man in their art and literature, the Romans were more concerned that theirs be practical, realistic, dignified and, often, grandiose. Roman artists were engineers. The Greeks gave us the idea of democracy, while the Romans codified it and institutionalized it. The Greeks were moderate in the conduct of their lives in contrast with the Romans. They found the idea of gladiators in the arena repugnant while Rome thrived on the games.

Yet, despite the excesses in public spectacles and in the courts of the emperors, the majority of Romans lived lives of austerity, self-discipline and order. They valued the law and their families, and those have been great bequests to people today who value them as well.

Cicero said that one would remain a child if he didn't know what happened before he was born. That is to say, he wouldn't grow in the knowledge of his ancestors or gain an understanding of history. At the former concentration camp in Dachau, Germany, a post-Holocaust sign admonishes visitors to remember history lest they repeat it. Hopefully, man can learn the good lessons of the past and build upon them, while he can also learn about the mistakes of the past and avoid repeating them.

Instructions for the Student and the Teacher

This book was designed for use by a student and a parent/teacher. Each student should have his own student book in which to write, and the teacher's guide should only be used by the teacher. The student book will facilitate writing the answers to the questions, and it will become a valuable resource for other high school and college classes.

Before reading the assigned books or chapters, the student should look over the group of questions relevant to the assignment so he can have an idea of what the reading will be about. He can jot down the answers to the questions as he comes across them in the reading. The questions are designed to assist the student in understanding the plots and events in the books, the character of the people in the stories, and the thoughts and ideas of the writers. The answers to the questions are found directly within the cited text, annotated with chapter numbers or line numbers, located above each cluster of questions or at the end of the questions. Please note: The numbers may not correspond exactly with editions other than those cited, but they are close from one edition to another. As the student reads and rephrases the answers to the questions he will be stimulated to think about other ideas relevant to the upcoming discussion with his teacher. The *Questions for Further Thought* are to facilitate discussion beyond the objective questions and answers. An additional help is the inclusion of research topics at the end of some of the readings. In addition, vocabulary words are listed when they are pertinent to understanding the text.

The question-and-answer method was chosen for the following reasons:

- It helps the student focus on detail. When a student reads a selection and then just reads a summary of that selection he is not challenged to stop and ponder the ideas and truths contained in all the words.

- It introduces the student in a small way to the method used by the ancient philosopher Socrates. This approach to learning is known as the Socratic Method and was used by this great teacher to help his students discover truth. He would ask questions and then respond to their answers with more questions. His goal was to find truth and the meaning of life and to help others discover them as well. Questioning, logical thinking and reasoning were his tools.

- It is a jumping-off point for discussion between the student and teacher.

It is my hope that the thought and discussion that arise from this book will lead a student and his teacher to a greater self-knowledge, a love of the ancients, and an understanding of the works at hand and their relevance today.

Please note: Unlike the answers to the objective questions, the answers to the *Questions for Further Thought* are the opinion of the author. They are presented to provoke thought and reflection. The reader may certainly come to different or additional conclusions.

Pronunciation Guide

Note: The following guide is to help the student pronounce Latin names and places which appear in the assigned texts. With the following exceptions, the letters are pronounced as in English. Unless written with an accent, Latin words are generally pronounced with the accent on the next-to-the-last-syllable.

Vowels	
A	as in father
E	as in set
I	as in machine
O	as in no
U	as in rule

Consonants, hard	before a, o, u, and au
C	as in cat
Cc	as in accord
Sc	as in ask
G	as in gas

Consonants, soft	before ae, e, oe, i
C	ch as in chin
Cc	tch as in match
Sc	sh as in ship
G	as in giant
Ti	when followed by a vowel becomes tsee as in tsetse fly
J	was not used in early Latin and is often changed to an "I" and pronounced as a "y"

Dipthongs	
Ae	a as in may
Au	ou as in mouse
Oe	ay as in day

SIGNIFICANT DATES IN ANCIENT ROME

B.C. (Before Christ)

Monarchy
753 Founding of Rome by Romulus
616-509 Rome rules by the Etruscan kings

Republic
509 Republic established with ouster of Estruscan king
494 Tribunate established
449 Law of the Twelve Tribes
390 Rome is sacked by the Gauls
312 Via Appia is built
268 First Roman silver coins
264-241 First Punic War with Carthage
240 Production of Tragedy and Comedy
218-201 Second Punic War
197 Rome defeats Philip V of Macedon
160 Cato's *Treatise on Agriculture*
149-146 Third Punic War, Carthage destroyed
112-106 War with Jugurtha
81 Cicero's first oration
73-71 Slave revolt led by Spartacus
60 First Triumvirate (Pompey, Caesar and Crassus)
58 Caesar's campaigns in Gaul
51 Caesar's *Commentaries on the Gallic Wars*
48 Civil War, Caesar defeats Pompey
46 Caesar appointed Dictator for 10 years
44 Cicero's Philippics against Mark Antony in command
43 Second Triumvirate (Octavian, Antony, Lepidus)
41 Sallust's Jugurthine War is published
37-30 Virgil's *Georgics* written
31 Antony and Cleopatra defeated at Actium
27 Pantheon built by Agrippa

Empire
27 Octavian as Augustus becomes Emperor
19 Virgil dies, *Aeneid* published

A.D. (Anno Domini, In the year of Our Lord)

c.4 Birth of Christ
8 Ovid exiled from Rome
14 Augustus dies, succeeded by Tiberius
17 Livy dies
43 Conquest of Britain begins
54 Nero becomes Emperor
64 Rome burns; persecution of Christians begins
70 Temple destroyed in Jerusalem
79 Mt. Vesuvius erupts; Pompeii and Herculaneum buried
79 Colosseum dedicated
121 Suetonius publishes *Lives of the Caesars*
122-127 Hadrian's Wall constructed
161 Marcus Aurelius becomes Emperor
212 Free inhabitants of provinces granted Roman citizenship
303 Persecution of Christians under Diocletian
313 Constantine grants toleration of Christianity
325 Council of Nicaea
330 Constantinople becomes capital of Empire
382 St. Jerome begins work on *Vulgate*
395 Roman Empire divided into East and West
410 Sack of Rome by Alaric, King of the Visigoths
413-426 St. Augustine writes *The City of God*
452 Attila the Hun persuaded not to sack Rome by Pope Leo I
455 Vandals sack Rome
476 Last Western Emperor deposed by Odoacer

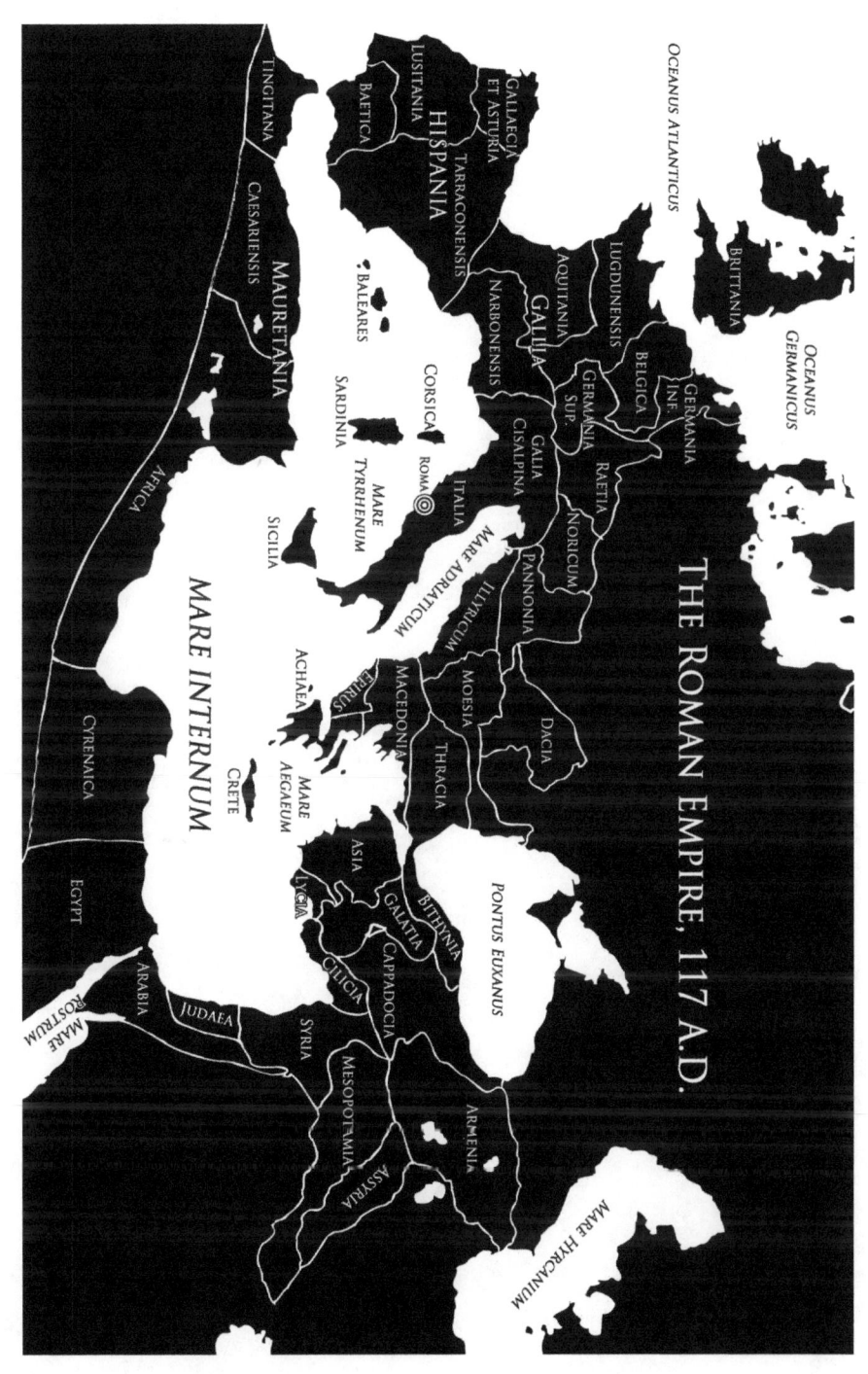

Poetry
Unit One

Unit 1: Poetry

The Aeneid

by Virgil
Translation: Robert Fitzgerald
Vintage Classics

Publius Vergilius Maro was born in 70 B.C. in Northern Italy near Mantua. His father was a landowner, some say a potter, and he had the resources to provide his son a good education. Virgil studied languages, medicine, law, rhetoric and all the other subjects that well-educated men studied. He became a protégé of Maecenas, a friend of Augustus, and was part of a group of poets known as Alexandrians who took their inspiration from third-century Greek poets. Maecenas encouraged Virgil to produce works that would please Augustus, and he composed rustic poems known as *Ecologues* and *Georgics*. These works were intended to instruct and also to encourage people to live the rural life of agriculture and to foster pride in their country. He was well-known by the age of 33 but uncomfortable with fame, so he spent most of his time away from Rome in Campania and Sicily.

Virgil did not seek the adulation of others and considered his fellow poets to be brothers. Many of them were mediocre and often claimed his work as their own. He sought to live virtuously in this regard, and he held no ill-feelings toward them.

From 30 to 19 B.C. Virgil wrote *The Aeneid*, the work for which he is most remembered. Augustus encouraged this work as a means to glorify Rome and the Empire. He never finished the work and had asked his friends to destroy it if he should die before completing it. Returning from Greece to his home, Virgil became ill and died. Augustus would not allow the manuscript to be destroyed, and it was published after his death.

Virgil was buried near Naples.

The Aeneid

The Aeneid is the Roman equivalent of the Greek epic poems *The Iliad* and *The Odyssey*, but it was also a response to what was happening politically in Rome at the time it was written. One-hundred years before Augustus there were civil wars. Augustus unified the state and restored peace, order, prosperity and civil happiness. He established an imperial form of government. Many Romans resented the fact that the old liberties of the Republic had been lost. Augustus is presented in *The Aeneid* to be descended from Aeneas, justifying full confidence in him as Emperor. In the story, Aeneas undergoes many hardships but consoles himself by remembering the great destiny of the nation he will found. He suppresses selfish needs for the greater good. *The Aeneid* influenced Romans to accept the monarch and the imperial system.

After the battle of Troy, most remaining Trojans were carried off to slavery. The story of the battle of Troy is found in Homer's *Iliad*. A small group of refugees escaped with Aeneas as their leader. Prophesies had said he would father a great nation. The small band wandered for seven years until they arrived in central Italy and settled in Latium where they fought a bloody war and were finally accepted. Aeneas married Lavinia, the princess of Latium. What had been many peoples, all at odds with one another, became one unified people. Romulus, a descendant of Aeneas, founded Rome.

There are some important themes to watch for. *The Aeneid*:
- is a national epic which illustrates the part Aeneas played in the founding of the Roman state and his embodiment of important Roman personal qualities - a sense of duty and responsibility
- views Rome as majestic and sacred, ordained by destiny to rule the world
- was written during the Golden Age - the reign of Augustus Caesar

It may be helpful to keep track of the primary gods:
- *Jove*: the chief Roman god, also known as Jupiter
- *Juno*: queen of the gods and wife of Jove
- *Aeolus*: god of wind
- *Neptune*: god of the sea
- *Amor*: Cupid, Desire, god of love
- *Pallas*: Athene, Minerva
- *Venus*: goddess of love, mother of Aeneas
- *Polyphemus*: Cyclops, one-eyed monster

Ausonia and Hesperia were names for Italy as Ilium was used for Troy.

A couple of common literary devices used in *The Iliad* and *The Odyssey* are also found in *The Aeneid*. Those are the simile, which is a comparison and begins with as...

> ...Turnus leapt and lunged on foot to closer quarters, as a lion after he sights from some high place a bull far off, spoiling for combat on the plain, goes bounding forward...
> *The Aeneid,* Book X lines 629-633

The other literary device is the epithet, which is a descriptive word or phrase and is used to define a character such as *fatherly Aeneas*, or *pitiless Achilles*.

The line numbers are for the Vintage Classics edition of *The Aeneid,* translated by Robert Fitzgerald. The line numbers may differ slightly in other versions.

Book I

(1-49)

1. How does the book begin?

2. What was Achilles' epithet?

3. Which goddess watched over Troy?

4. What did Juno hope for?

5. What was the mission of the Trojans?

(50-304)

6. What did Juno want Aeolus to do?

7. Why did the storm stop?

8. What did the Trojans eat once they landed safely?

9. In his speech to his companions, what did Aeneas promise?

(305-410)

10. Who interceded for Aeneas and his men?

11. How did Jupiter respond?

(411-894)

12. Whom did Aeneas meet when he went out exploring?

13. What did Venus tell Aeneas about this place?

14. As Venus led Aeneas and his companion toward the town, how did she disguise them?

15. What did Aeneas observe among the Tyrians?

16. Whom did Aeneas meet in the temple?

17. Whom did Aeneas see, but who couldn't see him?

18. What fatherly gesture did Aeneas perform?

Unit 1: Poetry

(895-1031)
19. Why did Venus disguise Amor as Ascanius?

20. How does Book I end?

Questions for Further Thought

A. What indication is there in the first book that Aeneas has superhuman qualities?

B. How do we know Dido's is an advanced civilization?

Book II

(1-80)
1. What was Aeneas' mood as he talked about Troy?

2. After building the horse, what trick did the Danaans (Greeks) play on the Trojans?

3. How did the "wiser" Trojans view the horse?

4. What was the Trojan view of the Greeks?

(81-272)
5. What did Sinon relate?

(273-729)
6. Why did the Trojans disregard the doom prophesied by Cassandra?

7. How did the Greeks enter the city?

8. What dream did Aeneas have while the Greeks were entering the city?

9. What did Aeneas say about the gods who had deserted Troy?

10. What did the aged Priam witness before his own death?

11. How did Priam reproach Pyrrhus?

12. How did Priam die?

(730-1046)
13. In the aftermath of the bloodbath, whom did Aeneas find?

14. What did he say about killing her?

15. Who stopped him from killing Helen?

16. What dilemma did Aeneas face?

17. What changed the mind of Aeneas' father?

18. Why couldn't Aeneas carry the gods?

19. What happened to Aeneas' wife Creusa?

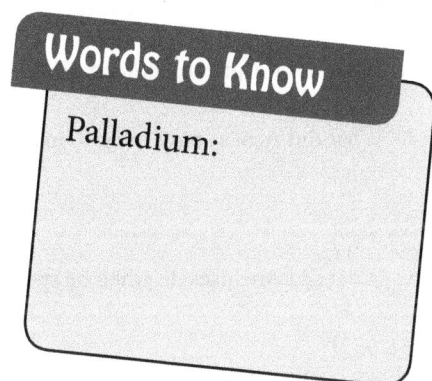

Words to Know

Palladium:

BOOK III

(1-101)
1. What did Aeneas call the people who left Troy with him?

2. When Aeneas pulled at the green shoots to find material for a roof, what did he find?

3. Why did Aeneas leave that place?

(102-265)
4. Where had Aeneas' family originated?

5. What happened after they began a new life in Crete?

6. What advise did Anchises give his son after Aeneas had conversed with the gods?

(266-373)
7. After three days of being stranded at sea, Aeneas landed at Strophades, only to find what?

8. What did Celaeno prophesy?

9. Whose island was Ithaca and what did Aeneas' people do as they passed it?

Unit 1: Poetry

(374-670)
10. Whom did Aeneas meet at Chaonia?

11. What sad story did she relate?

12. What did Aeneas request of Helenus?

13. What did the priest tell Aeneas?

14. What did Aeneas have to do to insure his safe arrival in Italy?

(671-757)
15. What did Anchises do when he spotted Italy?

(758-952)
16. What did Achaemenides relate to the Trojans?

17. Did Aeneas take Achaemenides with him?

18. What tragedy befell Aeneas at Drepanum?

Words to Know

Harpy:

suppliant:

QUESTIONS FOR FURTHER THOUGHT

A. What further indication do we have that Aeneas has a supernatural mission?

B. How has Virgil tied, without any doubt, his story of Aeneas to *The Odyssey* of Homer?

C. Why does Aeneas have so many trials?

D. What human qualities do you see in Aeneas?

BOOK IV

(1-126)
1. What was the queen's quandary?

The Aeneid

2. What advice did Anna give Dido?

3. What happened to Dido?

(127-499)
4. When Venus and Juno arranged for Dido and Aeneas to meet in the cave during the storm, Virgil says "That day was the first cause of death, and first of sorrow." What did he mean?

5. What rumor spread throughout the African cities?

6. What obligation was Aeneas neglecting?

7. What city did Mercury find Aeneas building?

8. After Mercury admonished Aeneas to get on with his mission, what was Aeneas' dilemma?

9. Dido was the one to bring up the subject of Aeneas' plans to leave. What were her concerns? What did Aeneas say of their "marriage?"

10. What change was seen in Aeneas?

(500-722)
11. What epithet was Aeneas given after Dido cursed him?

12. What did Dido plead for her sister to do?

13. What was the result?

14. Under what pretense did Dido have her funeral pyre built?

(723-978)
15. As Dido was preparing for her own death, what was Aeneas doing, and what did Mercury tell him?

16. What curse did Dido invoke on Aeneas?

17. How did Dido die?

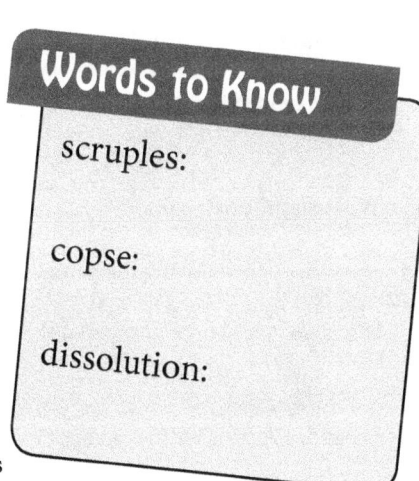

Words to Know

scruples:

copse:

dissolution:

Unit 1: Poetry

Questions for Further Thought

A. What values did Dido hold, as evidenced by her conversation with Anna?

B. Were the epithets given Aeneas fitting after what he had done?

C. What human traits do we see in Aeneas?

D. Is there a moral to this story of Aeneas and Dido?

Book V

(1-140)
1. How did the Trojans feel when they saw the fire of Dido's pyre from a distance?

2. Aeneas landed in Sicily where his father's ashes were buried. What did he do?

(141-368)
3. What was the first game?

4. What happened during the games that put winning above honor?

5. What was the source of most of the prizes Aeneas gave the competitors?

(369-627)
6. What did Aeneas tell the competitors about prizes?

7. After the dispute over who had won the foot race, what epithet was given Aeneas?

(628-777)
8. How did Ascanius, Aeneas' young son, participate in the games?

9. What would the skill Ascanius displayed that day later be used for?

(778-1014)
10. Why were the women unhappy?

The Aeneid

11. What were some of the traits of a goddess which revealed that the old woman was not Beroe?

12. What did the women do?

13. What died Nautes advise Aeneas to do?

(1015-1141)
14. What was to be the price paid for Aeneas to arrive in Italy, according to Neptune?

15. Whose life was it and how did he die?

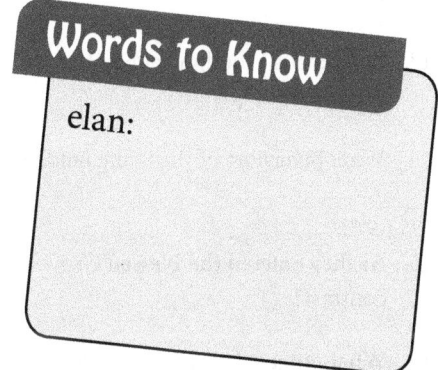

Words to Know

elan:

BOOK VI

(1-225)
1. When the Trojans landed at Cumae, what did Aeneas do while his men went foraging?

2. What did he promise Apollo?

3. According to the Sibyl, what awaited Aeneas in Italy?

4. What did Aeneas request?

5. What did Aeneas have to do before he could descend to the land of the dead?

(226-574)
6. What was the final thing Aeneas did in fulfilling the command of the Sibyl to bury his friend?

7. Who were some of the gods at the entrance to the cave?

8. What did Aeneas experience as he passed by these and other horrors?

9. Whose were the souls that Aeneas first encountered?

10. What did the Sibyl promise the soul of Palinurus?

(575-852)
11. How did Aeneas react when he saw Dido in the Field of Mourning?

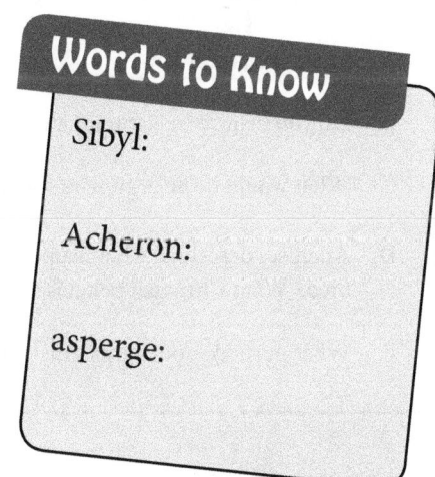

Words to Know

Sibyl:

Acheron:

asperge:

Unit 1: Poetry

12. When Aeneas and the Sibyl came to a fork in their way, what did she tell him about where the left fork led?

13. In Avernus Wood, what had the souls failed to do before they died?

14. What behaviors of the living landed them in this hell?

(853-972)

15. As they entered the Blessed Groves, what was the striking contrast?

16. What notable family was here?

17. What were some of the characteristics of the people who rested here?

Words to Know

disconsolate:

malefactor:

fasces:

(973-1222)

18. What happened to the souls of those who went to Lethe stream?

19. What vision did Anchises show Aeneas?

20. What would be the foundation of the city of Rome?

Questions for Further Thought

A. What is Natural Law?

B. Do you believe in Natural Law?

C. What would be an argument for Natural Law from reading this chapter of *The Aeneid*?

D. Anchises described what happened to the souls of those who were not purified before they died. What Christian belief is similar to what he described?

E. What purpose does Virgil's inclusion of Caesar Augustus in Anchises' vision serve?

Book VII

(1-138)
1. Where did the wild beasts on Circe's island come from?

2. Why did Virgil invoke the Muse at this point in his story?

3. Since Latinus had no sons, on whom did the destiny of Latium rest?

4. Who would be her husband?

(139-387)
5. What had Anchises told Aenéas long before?

6. When he realized he had arrived at the place of his destiny, what did Aeneas do?

7. What did Latinus tell Aeneas about his people?

8. What did Latinus realize as Aeneas' representative was speaking?

9. What gift did Latinus send to Aeneas?

(388-560)
10. What did Juno do when she realized she could not thwart the founding of Rome by Aeneas?

11. Whom did the Fury use to start the dissension?

(561-826)
12. What did the Fury goad Turnus to do?

13. How did he respond to her?

14. What happened next?

15. What started the battle?

16. How did the king respond to the strife?

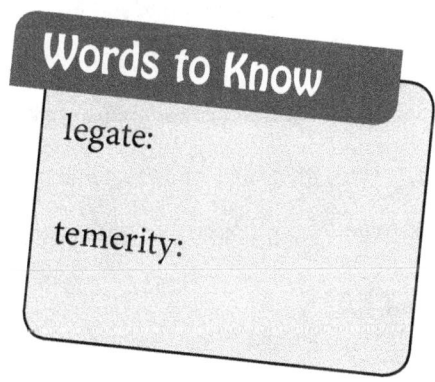

Words to Know

legate:

temerity:

(827-1122)
17. What sign did the Italians watch for to know that war was imminent?

18. Who opened the gates when Latinus refused to do so?

Unit 1: Poetry

19. Who responded to the call for war?

20. Who was Camilla?

Question for Further Thought

Do you think Latinus' refusal to declare war was a sign of weakness or strength? Explain your answer.

Book VIII

(1-247)
1. What sign would assure Aeneas that he was on the site of his city?

2. What would the city be called?

3. Who advised Aeneas to ally himself with King Evander of Pallas?

4. What sign of peace did Aeneas have as he approached Pallas?

5. What did Evander do to seal his pact with Aeneas?

(248-490)
6. What did Evander and Aeneas talk about at the feast?

7. What did Evander advise Aeneas?

8. What epithet did Virgil give Evander?

(491-792)
9. What gift did Venus promise Aeneas?

(793-992)
10. What was on the shield?

11. Did Aeneas know the history?

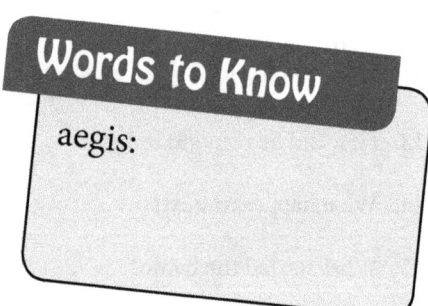

Words to Know

aegis:

Book IX

(1-240)
1. What instructions had Aeneas left the Trojans when he went to seek alliances?

2. What did Turnus order his troops to do in order to rout the Trojans?

3. How was the fleet saved?

(241-440)
4. What question did Nisus put to Euryalus about the Trojan's desire to fight?

5. What did Nisus request of Eurylaus in the event that he were killed?

6. What did Euryalus request of the Trojans on leaving to find Aeneas?

(441-638)
7. Why were the two men able to kill so many and remain unharmed themselves?

8. What mistake did Euryalus make?

9. What happened to the two Trojans?

(639-1130)
10. What did Virgil ask the Muse to help him do in this last section of Book IX?

11. What did Ascanius do before he shot his arrow at Remulus who was insulting his people?

12. What did Apollo in disguise tell Ascanius after he killed Remulus?

13. How did Turnus escape the Trojans?

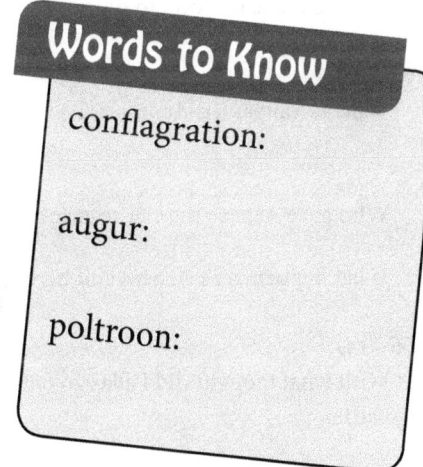

Words to Know

conflagration:

augur:

poltroon:

Unit 1: Poetry

Questions for Further Thought

A. What does Virgil mean that a soldier "lay undone by abundant Bacchus?"

B. What virtues were seen in Nisus and Euryalus?

Book X

(1-164)
1. What conflict did Jove predict when the gods converged to discuss the war between the Latins and the Trojans?

2. What did Venus ask of Jove?

3. How did Jove respond to Juno?

(165-296)
4. Who accompanied Aeneas as he returned to his people?

(297-605)
5. Who gave Aeneas the call-to-arms?

6. What happened as Aeneas and his entourage landed?

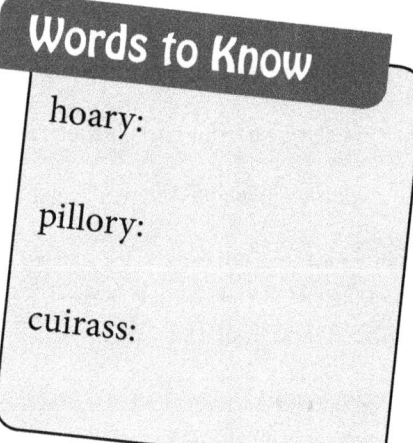

Words to Know

hoary:

pillory:

cuirass:

(606-714)
7. With what thought did Pallas go out to face Turnus in battle?

8. How did Jupiter respond to Hercules when Pallas prayed for his assistance?

(715-966)
9. What did Aeneas do when he arrived at the battle scene?

10. How did Jupiter respond to Juno's plea for Turnus?

11. What did Juno do?

The Aeneid

12. What happened to Turnus?

(967-1276)

13. Why did Aeneas not take a trophy from Lausus when he killed him?

14. What did Mezentius request of Aeneas before Aeneas killed him?

QUESTION FOR FURTHER THOUGHT

Why did Turnus lament his escape from death?

BOOK XI

(1-136)

1. The day after Aeneas killed Mezentius, what did he do?

2. What did he do with the body of Pallas?

3. What else did Aeneas send to Evander?

(137-286)

4. What did the Latins request of Aeneas?

5. How long was the truce between the Latins and the Trojans, and why did they have it?

(287-453)

6. How did the Trojans handle their dead?

7. What did Latinus acknowledge about why the Latins could not defeat the Trojans?

8. What did Latinus propose?

(454-721)

9. What did Drances propose?

10. Did Turnus agree?

Unit 1: Poetry

11. What role did Camilla play in the war?

(722-1032)
12. Who rode close to Camilla in war?

(1033-1240)
13. What distracted Camilla in battle?

14. What happened to Camilla?

15. What did Arruns do after he killed her?

16. What happened then?

17. As Book XI closes, what is the stage set for?

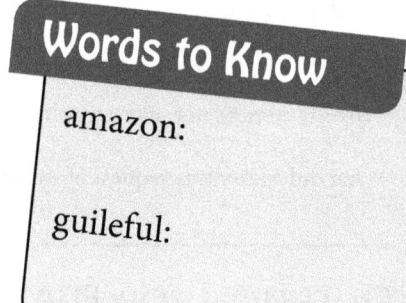

Words to Know

amazon:

guileful:

Questions for Further Thought

A. Who was the Mycenaean who met his death at his consort's hands that Venulus referred to when he was speaking to Latinus after he and the other emissaries returned unsuccessful from Diomedes?

B. Why was there no honor in killing Camilla?

Book XII

(1-157)
1. What did Latinus ask of Turnus?

2. What did Turnus propose?

3. Whose side was Amata the queen on?

(158-296)
4. What did Juno tell Turnus' sister?

The Aeneid

5. What did Aeneas' priest do before the fight?

6. What did Aeneas promise to do if defeated?

7. What did he promise if victorious against Turnus?

(297-444)
8. How did the Rutulians see the fight to come?

9. Who roused their spirits?

10. How was the pact broken?

11. How was Aeneas wounded?

(444-587)
12. How was he cured?

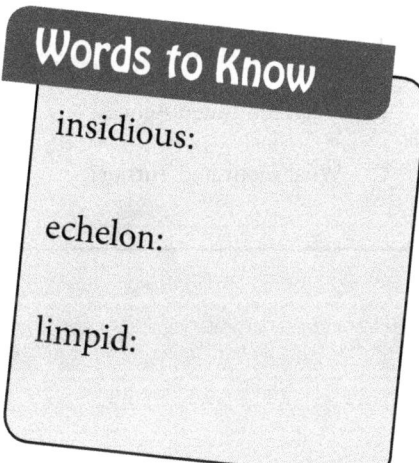

Words to Know

insidious:

echelon:

limpid:

(588-743)
13. What did Aeneas say to Iulus before he went back to face Turnus?

14. How did Aeneas treat his enemies differently than Turnus did?

(744-962)
15. What did Aeneas do to change the course of the battle?

16. What happened to the queen?

17. What did Turnus fear?

18. When Turnus arrived at the town, what happened?

(963-1068)
19. What happened to Turnus' sword?

20. How did Turnus respond?

21. What did Juno request of Jupiter when she realized Turnus' end was near?

22. What did Turnus ask of Aeneas after he was wounded?

23. What was the cause of Aeneas' final fury?

Unit 1: Poetry

Questions for Further Thought

A. What two epithets does Virgil give Aeneas in the early part of this book?

B. What motivated Aeneas?

C. What motivated Turnus?

Selections from The Metamorphoses

by Ovid
Translation: Horace Gregory
A Mentor Book

Ovid was born to an upper middle-class family in 43 B. C., a year after Caesar's assassination. As did many of his class, he studied rhetoric, Greek and Latin literature in Rome and philosophy and law in Athens. His brother was a lawyer and Ovid was as well, though his interest was in poetry, and serious lawyers could not be poets. He often amused his legal audiences by delivering his arguments in verse. After his brother died, he abandoned the law and dedicated his time to writing verse.
Ovid wrote many erotic poems and his first collection was published when he was about 23 years of age. His work was immediately popular with the Roman public. He fell from favor with Augustus in 8 A.D., was exiled from Rome, and his books were banned. It is not known for sure what he did to merit exile, but it separated him from his dedicated wife and family, though it did not result in his loss of property, which was a common punishment. He wrote copiously while in exile and much of his work reveals details of his life and state of mind. He died alone without ever having returned to Rome.

The Metamorphoses

The Metamorphoses (Transformations) was written before Ovid was sent into exile. It is a series of 250 stories from mythology, beginning with chaos and going through the time of Julius Caesar. The work influenced major poets such as Chaucer, Dante, Shakespeare, Milton and many great Renaissance painters as well. Before going into exile Ovid burned his copy of the work, but fortunately he had given copies to his friends who published it in his absence from Rome. He predicted at the end of the book that his name would be made immortal through it. He was correct as *The Metamorphoses* became the textbook of classical mythology.

Note to parents: *The Metamorphoses* deals with the mythological gods of ancient Greece and Rome, some of whom were very corrupt. The gods often overcame innocent virgins and impregnated them, leading to the birth of other mythological figures. I have tried to select stories which are not overly graphic in their descriptions of the lust of these gods, but I encourage parents and teachers to familiarize themselves with the material so they can determine what may or may not be appropriate for their students. Students should have a familiarity with mythology because it explains the beliefs of the people, and there are references to it in most classical literature and indeed, even in modern literary works. It also helps the students recognize references and phrases used in their everyday language.

Unit 1: Poetry

Book I

Chaos and Creation
1. Before everything was created, what was there?

2. Who calmed the elements?

3. What was missing from the created world?

4. What distinguished man from beast?

5. The first millennium was an age of what, and what were its characteristics?

6. What was the second age and what were its characteristics?

7. What was the third age and what were its characteristics?

8. What was the fourth age and what were its characteristics?

9. When Jove looked down, what did he feel?

10. What did he do?

The Flood
11. How did the gods feel?

12. What did Jove plan?

13. What happened?

Deucalion and Pyrrha
14. Who survived the flood?

15. What did they feel?

16. What did Deucalion and Pyrrha resolve to do?

17. What did Themis, the voice of fate, tell them to do?

18. Who was their mother. and what were her bones?

19. What happened when they obeyed?

The Metamorphoses

20. What happened next?

Apollo and Daphne
21. What was the newest creature?

22. What happened to Python?

23. What was Cupid's job?

24. What did he do?

25. What was her response?

26. What happened to her?

27. What symbol would Apollo wear?

Io and Jove
28. How did Jove betray Juno?

29. How did Juno know Jove was up to mischief?

30. What did Jove do when he was aware that Juno was near?

31. What did Juno do with Io?

32. How did Io reveal herself to her father?

The Pipes of Pan
33. How was Io saved?

Io as Isis
34. Who was Io's son?

35. What conflict did Epaphus have with his friend Phaethon?

36. Who was Apollo?

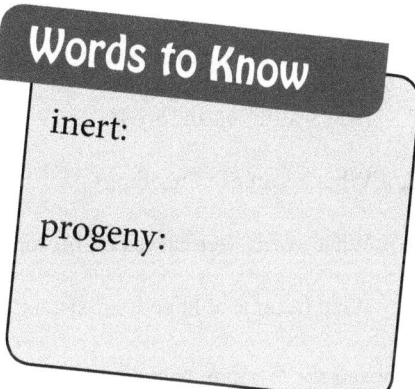

Words to Know

inert:

progeny:

Book II

Phaethon's Ride
1. Where did Phaethon go?

Unit 1: Poetry

2. What did Apollo reply to the question of Phaethon's paternity?

3. What did the boy request?

4. What did Apollo say about yielding to his son's wish?

5. What happened?

6. How did the Africans get black skin?

7. How was the earth saved?

8. What became of Phaethon?

9. What words were carved on his tomb?

10. What became of Phaethon's sisters?

Jove and the Arcadian Nymph
11. What was the story of Callisto?

Mercury and Herse
12. What traits did Mercury have?

13. Who was the war goddess?

14. How did Ovid describe Envy?

Words to Know

omnipotent:

usurp:

agility:

QUESTIONS FOR FURTHER THOUGHT

A. After reading some of the ancient beliefs about the gods, do you think they were admirable? Why or why not?

B. Was there another way that Apollo could have proven to his son that he was indeed his father rather than by "giving him the keys to the car?"

C. Is there a lesson here for those who want to do things they are not mature enough to do?

Book III

Cadmus

1. Why was Cadmus a pilgrim?

2. Did Cadmus find his sister?

3. What did the oracle tell him to do?

4. What happened?

5. At the end of the story of Cadmus, how does the poet let us know that Cadmus' happiness was not assured?

Actaeon

6. Why did Cadmus' grandson have antlers?

7. What danger did he face?

Semele

8. What appears to be the source of Juno's anger at Jove?

Tiresias

9. Could one god undo another god's work?

10. When Tiresias' sight was taken by Juno, what did Jove give him?

Echo and Narcissus

11. What prophesy did Tiresias give regarding Narcissus?

12. Who was Echo?

13. What happened to her?

14. Why was Narcissus cursed?

15. What did he love?

16. What became of Narcissus?

Unit 1: Poetry

Pentheus and Bacchus

17. Who alone disdained Tiresias' prophesies?

18. What did Tiresias predict?

19. What happed to Thebes?

20. In the tale told by Acoetes, who was the young lad found in a stupor?

21. The men broke a promise, took control of the ship away from Acoetes and set sail away from Bacchus' home of Naxos. What happened then?

22. What did Pentheus propose to do to Acoetes?

23. Did he die?

24. What became of Pentheus?

25. What was the lesson for the people of Thebes?

Words to Know

pilgrim:

shoal:

revelry:

Question for Further Thought

In which Greek play did Tiresias play an important part?

Book IV

Pyramus and Thisbe
1. Whom did the daughters of Minyas worship instead of Bacchus?

2. Who were Pyramus and Thisbe?

Ino and Athamas
3. Where did Juno go?

4. What did she want?

5. What "gifts" did the fury bring Ino and Athamas?

6. What did Ino do in her madness?

7. What became of them?

Metamorphosis of Cadmus
8. What became of Cadmus?

Perseus
9. Who was Acrisius?

10. What did Perseus want?

11. Why did Atlas refuse?

12. What did Perseus do as a result?

13. Where was Andromeda and why?

14. How did Perseus rescue her?

15. How did Perseus get Medusa's head?

16. Why did Medusa have snakes in her hair?

Words to Know

ambrosia:

truculent:

blasphemy:

Questions for Further Thought

A. Where does the story of Pyramus and Thisbe surface in later literature?

B. What are some of the virtues of the virgins mentioned by the poet in his descriptions?

Book V

Perseus' Battles
1. Why had Phineus come to the palace?

Unit 1: Poetry

2. What did her father tell him?

3. What happened?

4. How did Perseus resolve the fighting?

5. What did Phineus admit?

6. What became of Phineus?

Pallas Athena and the Muses
7. Who was Medusa's child?

8. What disturbed the peace and security of the muses?

Death and Proserpina
9. Why did Sicily have earthquakes and volcanoes?

10. What was the story of Proserpina?

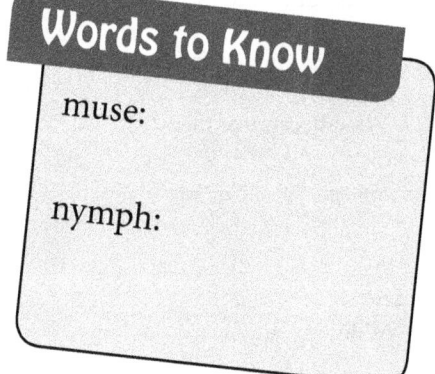

Words to Know

muse:

nymph:

Question for Further Thought

The ancient poets called on the muses for inspiration as they began their works. Can you name some famous works in which the muse was invoked?

Book VI

Arachne
1. What was Arachne's gift?

2. What advice did Arachne refuse to heed?

3. What was Arachne's "crime?"

4. What did Pallas and Arachne do?

5. When the two finished their weaving, what happened?

Niobe and Latona
6. From what did Niobe suffer?

7. What was the source of it?

8. Whom did she see as a rival for the people's affection?

9. What did Latona do?

10. How did they punish her?

11. What became of the seven daughters?

12. What became of Niobe?

Question for Further Thought

What is the lesson from the story of Arachne?

Book VII

Jason and Medea
1. What were Jason and his men (Argonauts) searching for?

2. Who was Medea, and what did she want?

3. Which won out, affection for her father or lust for Jason?

4. What happened in the forest when Medea and Jason met?

5. What happened in the arena?

6. How did Jason get the golden fleece?

7. How did Jason show love for his father?

8. What did Medea do?

Unit 1: Poetry

9. What evil thing did Medea do?

10. Who was Pelias?

11. What did Medea find when she returned home?

12. What did Medea do?

13. Who was Cerberus?

Minos Wars Against Aegeus
14. Why was King Minos trying to find allies to fight Greece?

15. Why could the sons of Aeacus not help King Minos?

16. Why were there no elderly faces to greet Cephalus?

The Myrmidons
17. What did Aeacus pray for?

18. Who were the Myrmidons?

19. What were some of the characteristics of the Myrmidons?

Caphalus and Procris
20. What was Procris' virtue?

21. What was magical about the javelin?

22. What kind of marriage did Cephalus and Procris have?

23. Why and how did Cephalus test his wife's loyalty?

24. Where did his javelin come from?

25. How did Procris die?

26. What happened as Procris died in Cephalus' arms?

Questions for Further Thought

A. After reviving Aeson, Medea left to practice her sorcery skills elsewhere, and she worked much evil. What might be the lesson here?

B. What famous warrior from *The Iliad* led the Myrmidons?

Book VIII

Minos, Nisus and Scylla

1. What was the conflict for Scylla?

2. Why did Minos have an honest cause for war?

3. What did Scylla resolve to do?

4. What did she take from her father Nisus while he slept?

5. What did she do with the plume?

6. What did King Minos do?

7. What was the result?

8. What happened to Nisus?

9. What happened to Scylla?

Daedalus and Icarus

10. What was Minos' son?

11. Who was Daedalus?

12. What did Daedalus want, and what did he do?

13. What happened to Icarus?

Words to Know

talisman:

hawser:

Unit 1: Poetry

Althaea and Meleager
14. What sorrow did Althaea have?

15. In her inner conflict between pride in her family heritage and motherly affection, which won out?

16. What did she decide to do?

17. What was the role of the furies?

18. Why did Meleager envy Ancaeus?

Baucis and Philomen
19. What is the moral of this story?

Book XI

Midas
1. How was Silenus described?

2. Why was Midas rewarded by Bacchus?

3. What did Midas ask as a reward?

4. Why was Midas unhappy?

5. What did Midas learn?

6. How was he cleansed of his guilt?

7. How did Midas change?

8. Why did Midas grow mule's ears?

The Building of Troy
9. Why was Laomedon punished?

10. How did Laomedon betray Hercules?

Sleep
11. Who are companions of Sleep?

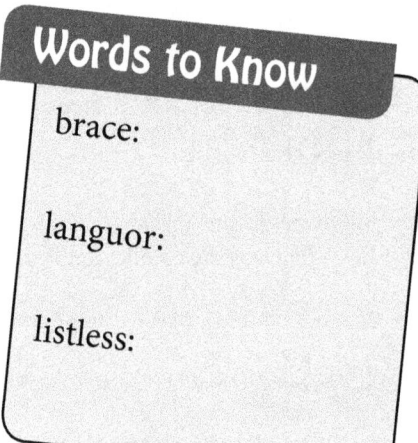

Words to Know

brace:

languor:

listless:

The Metamorphoses

Questions for Further Thought

A. After reviving Aeson, Medea left to practice her sorcery skills elsewhere, and she worked much evil. What might be the lesson here?

B. What famous warrior from *The Iliad* led the Myrmidons?

Book VIII

Minos, Nisus and Scylla
1. What was the conflict for Scylla?

2. Why did Minos have an honest cause for war?

3. What did Scylla resolve to do?

4. What did she take from her father Nisus while he slept?

5. What did she do with the plume?

6. What did King Minos do?

7. What was the result?

8. What happened to Nisus?

9. What happened to Scylla?

Daedalus and Icarus
10. What was Minos' son?

11. Who was Daedalus?

12. What did Daedalus want, and what did he do?

13. What happened to Icarus?

Words to Know

talisman:

hawser:

Unit 1: Poetry

Althaea and Meleager
14. What sorrow did Althaea have?

15. In her inner conflict between pride in her family heritage and motherly affection, which won out?

16. What did she decide to do?

17. What was the role of the furies?

18. Why did Meleager envy Ancaeus?

Baucis and Philomen
19. What is the moral of this story?

Book XI

Midas
1. How was Silenus described?

2. Why was Midas rewarded by Bacchus?

3. What did Midas ask as a reward?

4. Why was Midas unhappy?

5. What did Midas learn?

6. How was he cleansed of his guilt?

7. How did Midas change?

8. Why did Midas grow mule's ears?

The Building of Troy
9. Why was Laomedon punished?

10. How did Laomedon betray Hercules?

Sleep
11. Who are companions of Sleep?

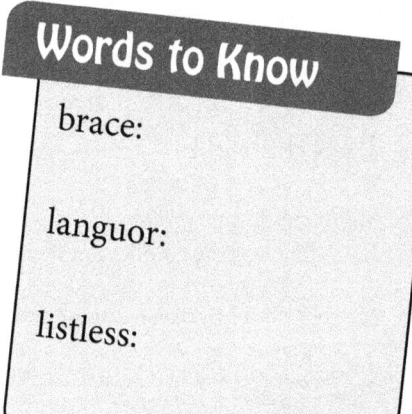

Words to Know

brace:

languor:

listless:

Question for Further Thought

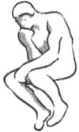

How do we know Midas was not a man of virtue?

Book XII

The Trojan War Begins

1. Why did the Trojan War begin?

2. What did the sign of the dragon eating the nine eagles mean?

3. What is the origin of lapis-lazuli?

4. When the seas were rough and hindering progress toward Troy, what did Agamemnon do?

5. What happens at the center of the Globe where Rumour lives?

6. Why were the Trojans ready for the advancing Greek army?

7. Did Achilles actually kill Cygnus?

The Death of Achilles

8. Who wanted Achilles dead?

9. Whom did he ask to kill Achilles?

10. Whose arrow did Apollo guide to kill Achilles?

11. What does Ovid say about Paris?

12. What would have been a better fate than being killed by Paris?

13. What does Ovid say about Achilles?

Words to Know

centaur:

armistice:

temerity:

Unit 1: Poetry

Questions for Further Thought

A. What does Ovid mean when he says of Agamemnon that the "politician over-ruled the father?"

B. What is more important: private virtue or public duty?

C. What great work tells the story of Achilles in detail?

Book XIII

The Dispute over Achilles' Armor

1. After Achilles died, what two men were in competition for his armor?

2. What did Ajax accuse Ulysses of?

3. What did Ajax use in his own defense?

4. Whom did Ajax say Ulysses abandoned in the war?

5. What kind of "hero" did Ajax say Ulysses was?

6. When did Ajax say Ulysses did his work?

7. What did Ulysses say in his own defense?

8. How did Ulysses say one's value to the world should be measured?

9. Why did Ulysses say he deserved the armor?

10. Who finally got Achilles' arms?

11. What did Ajax do?

The Fall of Troy

12. What happened to Troy?

13. What was the fate of the women of Troy?

14. What happened to Astynax, son of Priam?

The Sacrifice of Polyxena
15. Who was Polymestor?

16. What did the ghost of Achilles request?

17. Who was Polyxena?

18. How did she die?

Hecuba's Grief
19. What were some of the titles with which the women of Troy referred to Hecuba?

20. What did Hecuba lose?

21. When Hecuba went to fill her urn with water, what did she find?

22. What did Hecuba do to Polymestor?

Aeneas
23. Why did the Trojans have hope after the war?

24. What did Aeneas and the king of Delos do?

25. Where did the oracle tell Aeneas to go?

Book XIV

Circe, Glaucus and Scylla
1. What was Circe's talent?

2. Why did Circe use evil magic on Scylla?

3. What did she turn her into?

4. What did Scylla do in her rage?

Aeneas Visits Cumae
5. Whom did Aeneas meet on the shore of Africa?

Unit 1: Poetry

6. What did Aeneas do at Cumae?

7. What did he learn there?

8. How was Macareus (a Greek) rescued from the Cyclops at Aetna?

The Conquests of Aeneas
9. What was Aeneas' first conquest in Italy?

10. Whom had he fought?

11. What did Venus ask of Jove for her son Aeneas?

12. What did Ovid establish with Aeneas' immortality?

13. What did Ovid do in the reminder of Book XIV?

Book XV

Numa Hears the Story of Myscelos
1. Who succeeded Romulus as king?

2. What did Numa seek?

3. Why was Myscelos terrified?

4. Whom did Myscelos call upon when he was found guilty of trying to leave his home?

5. Did Hercules help him?

The Philosopher
6. Why did the Philosopher leave Samos?

7. What did the Philosopher say about meat?

8. What was the first age of man?

9. When man saw a lion kill and eat, what happened?

10. What does the Philosopher say about death?

11. To what does the Philosopher compare the four seasons of the year?

12. What was man's first tomb?

13. What are the four elements.

14. The meaning of the title of this work is summarized in Book XV. What did the author say about change?

Caesar
15. What gave Caesar his divinity?

16. What was Caesar's greatest triumph?

17. What was the name of the Trojan family from which Caesar descended?

18. Who was anxious with fear for her family?

19. What did Jove say about trying to protect Caesar?

20. Who was Caesar's son?

21. What would occur during his reign?

22. What became of Caesar's soul?

Epilogue
23. What did Ovid say about his work?

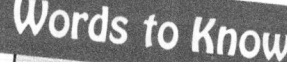

Words to Know

wraith:

Questions for Further Thought

A. What do the stories of Aeneas through Caesar establish?

B. What religion of today believes in reincarnation as expressed by the Philosopher?

C. What do Christians believe about death?

D. Was Ovid correct about his immortality?

Unit 1: Poetry

History
Unit Two

Unit 2: History

The Early History of Rome

by Livy
Translation: Aubrey de Sélincourt
Penguin Classics

Livy was born in Padua, Italy, sometime around 64-59 B.C. He studied philosophy and dedicated his life to writing his history of Rome. This work consisted of 142 books, 35 of which survive to the present day, and covers the period from Rome's founding to 9 B.C. Livy's purpose was to reconstruct and preserve a history of Roman heritage, to revive patriotism and restore Rome to its former civic virtue.

Livy was a champion of the Republican cause. He knew the Emperor Augustus who disapproved of his frank discussion of the recent past. This part of his work was not published until after Augustus' death. Livy saw the events of the story as related to the character, or moral fiber, of the people who lived through them; that being what influenced their actions and the resulting events. He used moral episodes to reveal what that character was. In his writing, the protagonists and antagonists usually give speeches or engage in dialogues at the climax of the episode to reveal what they are really like.

The Early History of Rome

Livy begins his work by saying that the failure of the Roman moral character has resulted in the present condition of Rome. Nevertheless, his pride in Rome's accomplishments is revealed, and he acknowledges the greatness that Rome had attained. He hoped that the study of history would result in the education of character, for in studying history, one could observe a variety of human experience and learn from the mistakes as well as the accomplishments of those who had gone before. Livy's work was popularly acclaimed in his own time.

Unit 2: History

Book I

(1200 B.C.-507 B.C.) Rome Under the Kings
1.1-1.60

1. How far back must Livy go to begin his history?

2. What does he say about the Rome of his day?

3. Why does he write of antiquity?

4. Why study history, according to Livy?

5. What virtues of Rome's past does Livy extol?

6. How has the situation changed?

7. Whom does Livy invoke for the telling of his story?

8. Which two Trojans were spared hostility from the Greeks after Troy fell?

9. According to legend, how did Aeneas end up in Larentum?

10. What is the legend of the founding of Rome?

11. After performing religious rites, what did Romulus do?

12. How did he populate his town?

13. Whence the term patrician?

14. How did Romulus attempt to find women for his town?

15. What happened at the festival in honor of Neptune?

16. How did Romulus reassure the Sabine women?

17. How was the fight between Rome and the Sabines settled?

18. How does Livy describe Romulus and his reign?

19. How did Romulus supposedly die?

20. How did Proculus calm the crowd who blamed the senators for Romulus' death?

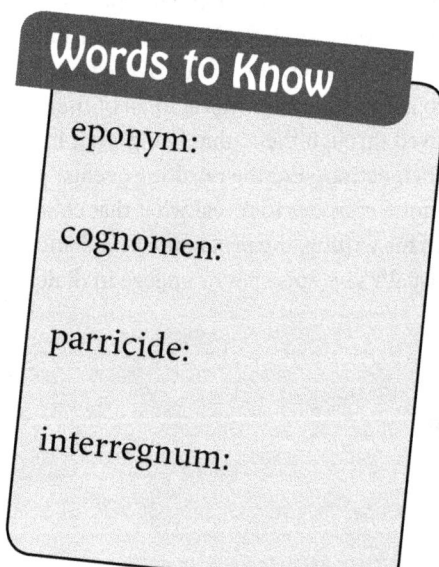

Words to Know

eponym:

cognomen:

parricide:

interregnum:

The Early History of Rome

21. What conditions existed after Romulus died?

22. Who was elected king?

23. For what second beginning did Numa hope?

24. What was the significance of the Temple of Janus?

25. What was Numa's first act?

26. On what authority did he establish religious rites and offices?

27. What was the result of this leadership?

28. How long did Numa reign?

29. How were the reigns of Romulus and Numa compared?

30. How was the conflict between Alba and Rome settled?

31. What did Livy say about the killing of Mettius who had led Alba to desert Rome?

32. Once defeated, what was the procedure for bringing Alba into Rome?

33. How did Tullus die?

34. How did Tarquin acquire the throne?

35. What architectural accomplishments are credited to Tarquin?

36. For what is Servius remembered?

37. What did Livy say about the relationship between the younger Tullia and her sister's husband Tarquin?

38. What was the result of their partnership?

39. What was Tarquin's driving force?

40. How is the reign of Servius remembered?

41. Why did Sextus Tarquinius want Lucretia?

Words to Know

pontifex maximus:

vestal virgins:

brigand:

sacrilege:

Unit 2: History

42. Why did Lucretia kill herself?

43. What was said about her innocence?

44. What did Brutus do?

45. What ended at this time?

Questions for Further Thought

A. How would you characterize Tarquin?

B. Does Christianity agree with the answer in 43?

Book II

(507 B.C. - 468 B.C.) The Beginnings of the Republic
2.1-2.60

1. Livy wrote about patriotism. What did he say?

2. What benefit did Rome enjoy as a result of the long years of the monarchy?

3. What was the primary difference between kings and consuls?

4. What did the rods signify?

5. What was the difference between "Fathers" and "conscripts?"

6. What happened to the Tarquins?

7. Why did the aristocracy revolt against the new government?

8. While the Tarquin envoys were back in Rome to secure their property, what did they do? (2.4)

9. Who were the most notable conspirators with the Tarquins?

10. What happened to the conspirators?

The Early History of Rome

11. When treachery failed, what did the Tarquins plan?

12. What happened when the forces of the Tarquins and Rome met?

13. What great tribute did Brutus receive?

14. What contribution did the poor make in exchange for food and exemption from tolls and taxes when the Etruscans blockaded the city?

15. How did Horatius hold off the Etruscans who attacked Rome?

16. What did the Etruscans led by Porsena do next?

17. What did Gaius Marcias do?

18. What did Porsena do?

19. Why was a dictator appointed?

20. What was the significance of a dictator?

21. What plight did many soldiers suffer?

22. What two threats did the country face during this time?

23. What did the consul Servilius do?

24. Why was Valerius welcomed as a dictator by the commoners?

25. Why did he leave office?

26. Whom did the senators choose as their spokesman to the commoners?

27. What purpose did his fable about the revolt of the body parts against the belly serve?

28. What did Coriolanus think about the commoners?

29. What became of Coriolanus?

30. With whom did he plot war?

31. What did Tullius tell the consuls?

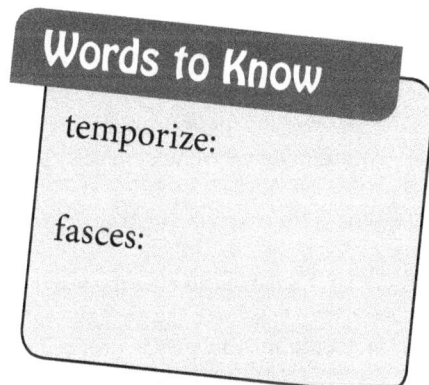

Words to Know

temporize:

fasces:

Unit 2: History

32. What did the senate do as a result?

33. What did Tullius incite the people to do?

34. Who commanded the army in this engagement?

35. How did the Roman commoners want the consuls to respond to the threat?

36. How did Marcius respond?

37. What did the women of Rome do?

38. What did Marcius do after his mother spoke for Rome?

39. What was the "poisonous disease of wealthy and powerful communities, the one destructive influence which brought mighty empires low?"

40. Why is the triumph after the defeat of the Etruscans so well remembered?

41. What did Fabius do after the war?

42. What did the Fabian clan propose to the senate?

43. What happened to the Fabii?

44. What issue kept reappearing whenever Rome was free from outside conflicts?

45. What did the ex-consuls Furius and Manlius tell the young nobles?

46. How did Appius deal with the soldiers under his command against the Volscians, and what was the result?

47. How did Quinctius deal with his men against the Aequians?

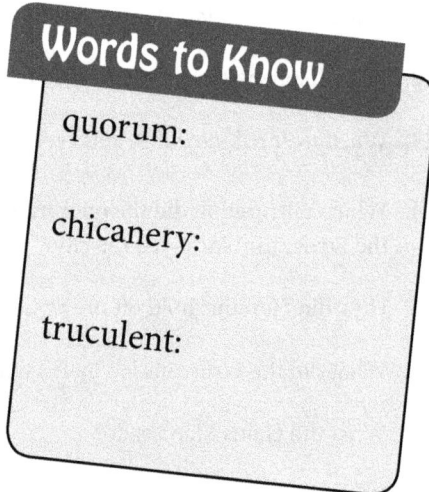

Words to Know

quorum:

chicanery:

truculent:

The Early History of Rome

QUESTIONS FOR FURTHER THOUGHT

A. Do you agree with the young aristocrats who believed that it was impossible to live "in pure innocence" under the law? Explain your answer.

B. What happens when people disregard laws and influence those in power?

BOOK III

(467 B.C. - 372 B.C.) The Patricians at Bay
3.6-3.69

1. What rendered Rome helpless against invaders?

2. What did the senate command the people to do?

3. What generally followed successful conclusions of wars?

4. What did Terentillus propose?

5. What was the difference between a triumph and an ovation?

6. Who was Verginius?

7. What was the first record of a bond being paid to assure a defendant would appear for trial?

8. Did Caeso appear?

9. How did the patricians avoid the legislation wanted by Terentillus?

10. Who was Herdonius?

11. During the slave uprising, what did Valerius the consul promise the people?

12. How did the people respond?

Words to Know

tribune:

patricians:

plebians:

consuls:

Unit 2: History

13. What was the result of the attack on the Citadel?

14. How did Cincinnatus castigate the senate?

15. According to Cincinnatus, when did the gods smile on Rome?

16. Quinctius scolded the senate for wanting him to be consul for a second consecutive term. What was his argument against this?

17. What was Cincinnatus doing when he received an envoy from the city?

18. What did the envoys say to him?

19. Why did the soldiers have to each carry 12 stakes?

20. What was the significance of passing "under the yoke?"

21. How long was Cincinnatus Dictator and why?

22. Why were three representatives sent to Athens?

23. Three-hundred and two years after Rome was founded, its government changed for the second time from kings to consuls and now to what?

24. What was the code of laws called which was adopted during this time?

25. Why did the *decemvirs* encourage the citizens to read the proposed laws?

26. What happened after the first *decemvirs* had served their term?

27. Did the *decemvirs* prove to be good field commanders? Why?

28. After whom did Appius lust?

29. What did Appius propose?

30. Who stood up for her in her father's absence?

Words to Know

tutelary god:

circumvallation:

sacrosanct:

Sibylline Books:

cohort:

31. How did Verginius set his daughter free?

32. Why did he kill her?

33. After the commons left Rome, they made demands on the senate. What were they?

34. How did the senate respond?

35. After the elections, what laws were passed?

36. What was ironic about Appius' conduct when he was brought to trial?

37. What became of Appius?

38. Once things settled down in Rome, what did the consuls do?

39. These battles resulted in victories for Rome. What was unique about the triumphs for the consuls Valerius and Horatius?

40. The consul Quinctius spoke about the advance of the enemy on Rome. To what did he attribute the enemy's boldness?

41. What was the result of Quinctius' speech?

Questions for Further Thought

A. The Roman people wanted to have their basic rights assured. Our basic rights are assured through our Constitution and its Amendments. What is the First Amendment to the US Constitution?

B. Do you think our senators, congressmen or presidents should serve successive terms? What are the advantages? What are the disadvantages?

C. The Romans did not mark the years as we do today (9 B.C. or 1950 A.D.). How were the years identified?

D. Class struggles were endless. What were the two classes always in conflict?

Unit 2: History

Book IV

(445 B.C. - 404 B.C.) War and Politics
4.1-4.14

1. Why did the senators object to the bill proposed by the tribune Canuleius legalizing marriage between the classes and election of the consuls from either party?

2. What did the aristocrats often do to avoid discussion of unpopular proposals by the commons?

3. What was the argument against intermarriage?

4. Was the ban on intermarriage lifted?

5. What decision was reached regarding military tribunes?

6. What was the meaning of "censorship?"

7. What was the cause of the civil war in Ardea which forced the aristocrats of Ardea to seek help from Rome?

8. What was the result?

9. Why was Quinctius Cincinnatus appointed Dictator for a second time?

10. What qualities did the senate see in Cincinnatus, who by this time was old and certainly reluctant to bear the burden of office?

11. What happened to Maelius?

Questions for Further Thought

A. Canuleius said that marriage had always been a private arrangement between families and that they were now going to be subjected to the restraint of laws which divided the society. Does the state have a valid interest in the institution of marriage? Why?

B. What are the unifying elements in this work?

C. Is it ever wise to have somebody in power who is above the law?

D. What was the role of Cincinnatus and future dictators?

Book V

(403 B.C. - 386 B.C.) The Capture of Rome
5.1-5.55

1. What radical decision was made in Rome when Veii elected a king and the Romans realized the Etruscan communities were considering aid to Veii?

2. What city, besieged for 10 years by united Greek armies for the sake of a woman, was Appius Claudius referring to when speaking to the commons among whom dissent was fomented by the tribunes?

3. What virtue was he calling for in having the soldiers see the war through, postpone their plans, wait to fulfill their desires and endure winter?

4. What unexpected disaster took place soon after?

5. What was the unexpected result?

6. With all the volunteers, was the campaign successful?

7. What was the significance of the draining of the Alban Lake?

8. What did the Commander Camillus vow to Juno if he was victorious?

9. How did the Romans surprise the Veintes?

Unit 2: History

10. What did the tripping of Camillus during prayer portend?

11. What behavior was recorded in the men who removed the property of the gods?

12. What benefit did the women of Rome receive when they gave up their gold ornaments for Apollo?

13. How did Camillus show strength of character in dealing with Falerii?

14. What is the story about the honest pirate?

15. What message of doom was ignored?

16. What other unfortunate event took place?

17. The Gauls had been moving south for many years. How did they learn about Rome? (5.36)

18. What did the Gauls demand?

19. How did the Gauls respond when the envoys asked by what sort of justice they demanded the land?

20. Why did the focus turn from Clusium to Rome?

21. When the Gauls complained about the incident and demanded that the Fabii surrender, how did the senate respond?

22. What did Livy say about destiny?

23. How did Livy characterize the Gauls?

24. What was the advantage of the Gauls as they met the Roman army?

25. How did the Roman army behave when it confronted the Gauls?

26. How did Livy describe the Gauls at the gates?

27. What did the Romans do when the Gauls entered the gates?

28. How did the nobles and old senators face their deaths?

29. Did the Gauls launch an immediate assault on the city?

30. What happened when the Gauls finally stormed the citadel?

The Early History of Rome

31. Why was the siege unsuccessful?

32. What did Camillus do?

33. How did the Gauls react when Gaius Fabius Dorsuo performed the annual animal sacrifice on the Quirinal?

34. Why couldn't the gathering army at Veii just appoint a general?

35. What did the senate do?

36. During an undetected surprise attack by night on the citadel, what saved it?

37. What was happening as Camillus entered Rome?

38. What did the Romans have in their favor?

39. What was the outcome of the military engagement?

40. What privilege did the women receive when they gave up their gold to pay off the Gauls?

41. After fulfilling his religious duties, what was Camillus' next important task?

42. To what did Camillus attribute the present disaster?

43. Besides the sin of abandoning the sacred places in moving to Veii, what other concern did Camillus express?

44. How old was Rome at this point?

45. Were the people convinced to stay?

46. What settled the matter?

47. How did Livy describe the reconstruction?

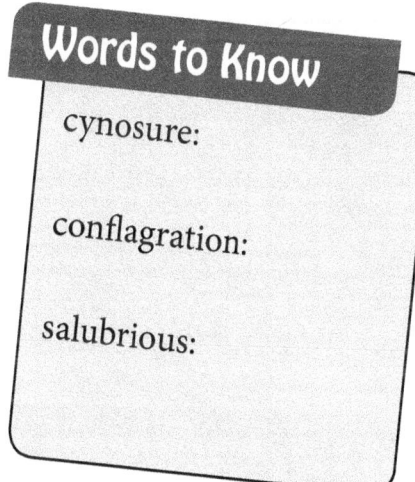

Words to Know

cynosure:

conflagration:

salubrious:

53

Unit 2: History

Questions for Further Thought

A. Livy described the Gauls as superstitious. Were the Romans also superstitious? What does superstitious mean? Explain your answer.

B. Is it just to leave the "aged and useless" to die in the interest of saving the younger "useful" among us? Why? Explain your answer.

C. By leaving the "aged and useless" to die, what does that tell you about the Roman view of valuable life?

The War with Hannibal

by Livy
Translation: Aubrey de Sélincourt
Penguin Classics

This work consists of Books XXI-XXX of the *History of Rome from Its Foundations* by Livy. It covers the 17 years of the second war between Rome and Carthage. During that time Rome suffered huge disasters before finally triumphing over Carthage. These wars between Rome and Carthage are known as the Punic Wars.

I suggest having the student memorize the opening poem by Juvenal, *Satire*, lines 147-167.

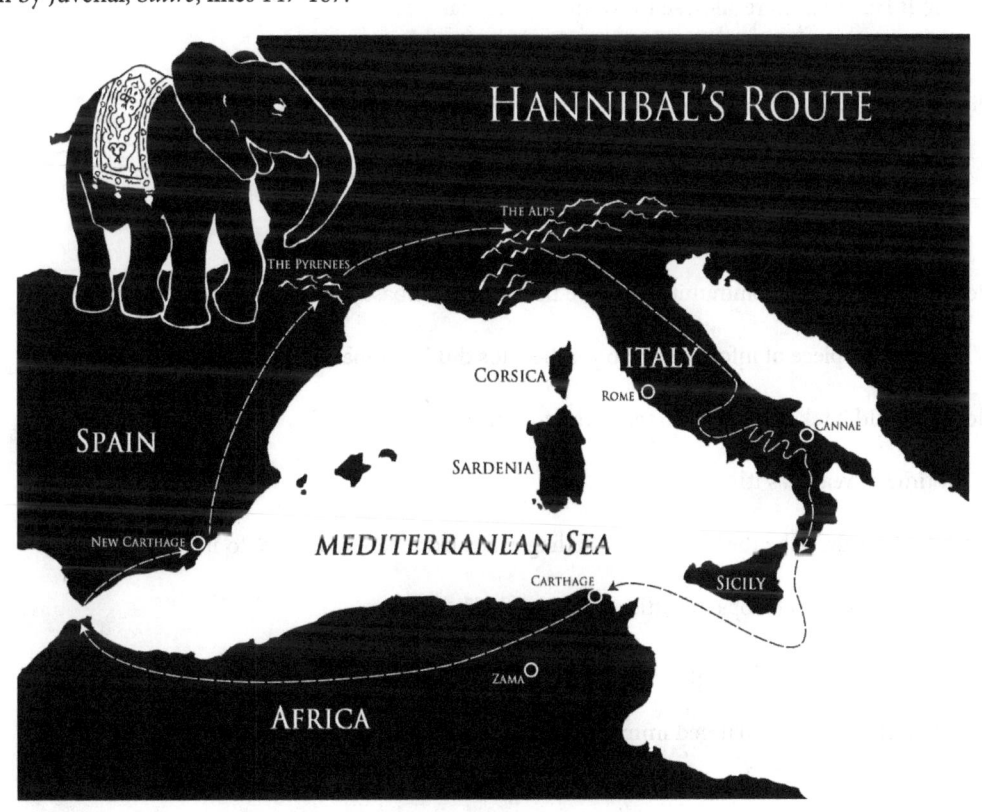

Unit 2: History

BOOK XXI

(218 B.C.)
(1-53)

1. What contributed to the unique character of the war between Rome and Carthage?

2. Why did Hanno not want the young Hannibal to be present with the troops?

3. Did Hanno's views prevail?

4. What traits did Hannibal manifest early on?

5. What were Hannibal's vices?

6. What year did Saguntum seek aid from Rome?

7. What did Hanno warn the Carthaginian senate would happen if Hannibal were allowed to continue the assault on Saguntum and the Roman envoys ignored?

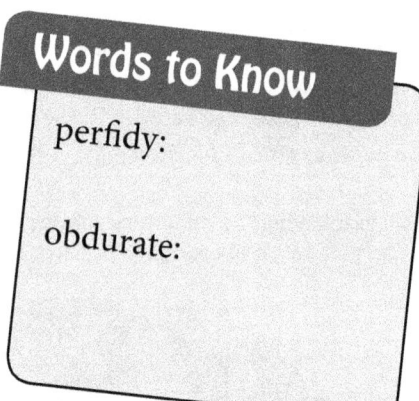

Words to Know

perfidy:

obdurate:

8. Did the senate support Hanno?

9. What was the fate of Saguntum?

10. What did Rome realize after the fall of Saguntum?

11. How did the Spanish communities receive the Roman embassy seeking alliance with Rome?

12. What valuable piece of information about the Alps did Hannibal receive from his Gallic guides?

13. How long did it take Hannibal to reach the summit?

14. What time of year was it?

15. How did Livy describe the trek of the Carthaginians from New Carthage to Italy?

16. Who led the Roman troops in battle with Hannibal?

17. Who saved Scipio in his unexpected first meeting with Hannibal?

18. Who was the consul who urged immediate action against Hannibal while Scipio urged delay?

Book XXII

(216 B.C.)
(44-50)

1. At Cannae, what was the problem with Roman leadership?

2. What disadvantage did the Romans have which Hannibal exploited?

3. How did Hannibal know the Romans were beaten?

4. How many of the 50,000+ soldiers got away after the battle?

Book XXIII

(216 B.C.)
(1-33)

1. Hannibal had crossed the Alps and had a major success at Cannae against the Romans. Did he head straight for Rome?

2. Livy said life in Capua had always been soft and luxurious. What did he attribute that to?

3. What danger did this softness pose for Rome?

4. What had Rome done to guarantee Capua's loyalty?

5. Who was Decius Magius?

6. According to Livy, what tactical error did Hannibal make at Capua which robbed his army of its vigor?

7. Whom did Philip of Macedon side with and why?

8. What treachery did Philip engage in?

Question for Further Thought

Was Hannibal successful in making alliances with non-Roman Latins? Why?

Unit 2: History

Book XXVI

(211 B.C.)
(1-50)

1. What was going on at Capua?

2. How close to Rome did Hannibal make camp?

3. Did Hannibal remain at Capua to defend it?

4. How did the Romans punish the Numidians caught spying?

5. What did Virrius offer the leaders of Capua?

6. What did the majority agree to do?

7. What was the fate of Capua?

8. Who finally came forth to take the position of pro consul for Spain?

9. Why did the Romans entrust such a young man with the position?

10. Why did Livy praise the olden times?

11. What did Scipio state his purpose in Spain was?

12. How did Scipio begin his operations?

13. Why was New Carthage important?

14. How did Scipio get into New Carthage?

15. How long did it take for Scipio to take New Carthage?

16. What did Scipio do the day after taking New Carthage?

17. What precedent did Laelius want to avoid?

18. Why did Livy hesitate to state the numbers of hostages?

19. How did Scipio treat the hostages and prisoners?

20. What did Scipio say to Allucius?

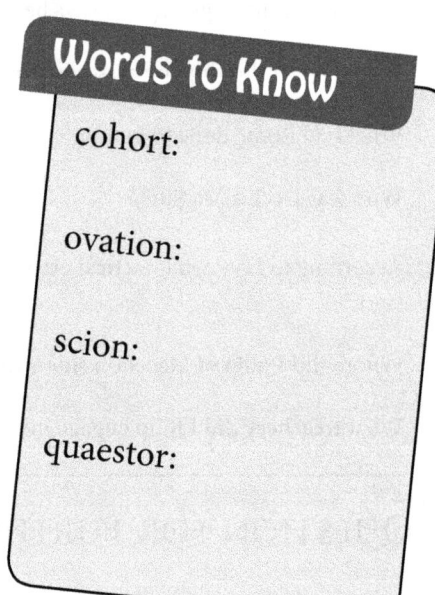

Words to Know

cohort:

ovation:

scion:

quaestor:

The War with Hannibal

 QUESTIONS FOR FURTHER THOUGHT

   A. What was the significance of the place names Trebia, Trasimine and Cannae?

   B. Why was the loss of New Carthage such a blow to Carthage?

BOOK XXVIII

(207-205 B.C.)
(16-40)

1. Who expelled the Carthaginians from Spain?

2. When did this occur?

3. What were Scipio's plans next?

4. Who was Syphax?

5. How did Syphax come to mediate a settlement between Hasdrubal and Scipio?

6. What was Scipio's reason for attacking Iliturgi?

7. How would you describe the unrest following news of Scipio's illness and rumors of his death?

8. What did Scipio say about Coriolanus when he was speaking to the leaders of the mutiny?

9. How did Scipio deal with the mutineers?

10. What other Scipio family members had connections to Spain before Publius Scipio?

11. Who was Masinissa?

12. What reward did Scipio receive when he returned to Rome after his triumph in Spain?

13. For what reason did Scipio say he had been elected consul?

14. Why did Quintus Fabius Maximus think Scipio should stay in Italy rather than go to Africa?

Unit 2: History

15. Did the senate decide to allow Scipio to go to Africa?

Book XXIX

(205 - 203 B.C.)
(1-34)

1. What was Scipio's ruse in raising Sicilian troops?

2. Was Scipio the first of the Romans to arrive in Africa?

3. Why and how did Hasdrubal secure Syphax's alliance in his war with Rome?

4. What did Scipio do before he sailed to Africa with his fleet?

5. What was Scipio's stated purpose in this campaign to Africa?

6. Why was Carthage vulnerable to the arrival of Scipio?

7. Who appeared to help Scipio?

8. What did Scipio do with the plunder, men and cattle that his men gathered in battle?

Words to Know

dilatory:

audacity:

cognomen:

quinquennial:

Book XXX

(203 - 201 B.C.)
(5-44)

1. When Scipio's men set fire to the huts of Syphax's troops, to what did the Numidians and then the Carthaginians attribute the fires, and how did they respond?

2. What happened to Hasdrubal and Syphax?

3. When Masinissa entered Cirta with Syphax in chains, what did Syphax's wife beg for?

4. What did Masinissa do?

5. What happened to Syphax?

6. What excuse did Syphax give Scipio for abandoning their pact of friendship?

7. What virtue did Scipio pride himself in?

8. How did Masinissa solve his dilemma?

9. With what words did she die?

10. How did the Carthaginians respond to news of the capture of Syphax?

11. What did Scipio demand of the envoys?

12. On what did Hannibal blame his defeat?

13. What mistake did Hannibal acknowledge making?

14. What did the older senators note about how people saw blessings and defeats?

15. By the time Hannibal left Italy, how many years of the war had passed?

16. What did Hannibal ask Scipio for when they met in the open field between both of their armies?

17. Did Scipio agree?

18. How many elephants did Hannibal place in his battle line?

19. How was Hannibal's army described?

20. In the decisive battle between Hannibal's and Scipio's forces, what was the result?

21. What happened to Hannibal?

22. What did Hannibal say about peace in a great country?

23. What did Livy say about the surname Africanus?

Unit 2: History

Questions for Further Thought

A. In your opinion, was Hannibal a great general? Why or why not?

B. In your opinion, was Scipio a great general? Why or why not?

C. Do modern people have the staying power to remain at war for such protracted periods as we saw in the study of Ancient Rome? Why?

The Conspiracy of Catiline

by Sallust
Translation: S.A. Handford
Penguin Classics

Sallust was born in central Italy in 86 B.C., served as a *quaestor* and at the age of 31 became a tribune. He sought the condemnation of Milo who was being defended by Cicero for the murder of Clodius. Clodius had ties to Caesar so Sallust was seen as an enemy of the senators, of whom Caesar was a leader. However, a few years later, Caesar's influence gained Sallust a second quaestorship, and he had the opportunity to serve Caesar as proconsular governor of Africa Nova. His actions were not admirable, and he retired as a rich man, due to shamelessly plundering the province and bribing Caesar. He spent his retirement writing and finally died around 35 B.C.

Not much remains of Sallust's works. The primary works we have, *The Conspiracy of Catiline* and *The Jugurthine War*, were admired by such notables as Quintilian, Tacitus, St. Jerome and St. Augustine. Like most ancient historians, Sallust wrote with a bias and took pleasure in his work as a literary creation, important as much or more so for its literary qualities as for its scholarship. History was seen as a branch of epic poetry used to please the audience, as instruction in the traditions of the people and as a branch of rhetoric and philosophy. It was to inspire by presenting great men and their actions, to preach about the consequences of vice, and to gain sympathy for one cause or the other. Sallust is said to have chosen Catiline because his story was a prime example of wickedness which threatened the security of Rome.

The Conspiracy of Catiline

The Conspiracy of Catiline took place 42 years after the Jugurthine War. Rome was involved in serious wars against German invaders and Mithridates, a king from Asia Minor. Her Italian allies were rebelling against unjust treatment at her hands. The slaves were in revolt and Rome was engaged in a civil war. Sulla seized power and was the first military dictator of Rome, commanding legions composed of landless volunteers. Marius had reorganized the legions into ten cohorts, which were groups of 600 men, secured good equipment for them, and cultivated good morale among the soldiers. He created an efficient army this way and realized many victories in the field. He defeated the Germans, but had little wisdom and ended up a political failure.

Problems were brewing in Italy because the majority of Italians were excluded from Roman citizenship. Sulla became consul in 89 B.C., and he was given command in Asia in an impending war against Mithridates. However, a tribune named Publius Rufus conspired to have that command transferred to Marius. Sulla marched with his legions and secured his command while Marius fled to Africa. Back in Rome, however, Marius returned from Africa and seized command of the city and slaughtered Sulla's allies. Soon after, Marius died, and Sulla returned to Rome. He was appointed dictator "to draw up laws and settle the constitution of the Republic." He had unlimited powers, restored the senate to its former authority, curtailed the powers of the tribunes, and reorganized the administration of criminal justice. He failed to curb the power of successful generals, and the constitution was threatened as a result. The courts were soon changed by the consuls Crassus and Pompey, the tribunes were restored to power, and the senate once again diminished in power.

Catiline, who was once supported by Crassus and possibly Caesar, ran for the consulship in 63 B.C. He had the reputation of a bloodthirsty killer and after his defeat became a revolutionary. Cicero was a bitter enemy and had been instrumental in his defeat. Catiline conspired to make war on Rome. Cicero was the consul, and his use of authority was judged as too harsh. The conspirators were caught and put to death.

Chapter 1

Preface
(1-10)

1. According to Sallust, what powers should we use in the pursuit of fame?

2. What does he say is the function of the body?

3. In ancient times, what controversy was settled and by whom?

4. What vices are common to men?

5. How does a man get satisfaction in life?

6. What happened when Sallust involved himself in politics?

7. What does he say of Catiline?

8. What was the form of the early government of Rome?

9. After the constitutional monarchy, what form of government evolved?

10. What was the difference in attitude between the Greeks and Romans toward historians?

11. How does Sallust describe the period of the consuls?

12. What began the downfall of Rome?

13. What does Sallust say about ambition?

14. What does he say about avarice?

15. What mistake had Sulla made?

Chapter II

Catiline's First Attempts at Revolution
(13-23)

1. Whom did Catiline seek to befriend?

2. What act of Catiline's tortured him?

Unit 2: History

3. What did Catiline do with the youths?

4. What conditions existed in Rome as Catiline planned a revolution?

5. What did Catiline say in his speech to his supporters?

6. What prizes did he promise them?

7. What made the people vote for Cicero instead of Catiline for consul?

Words to Know

oligarchy:

proscription:

QUESTIONS FOR FURTHER THOUGHT

A. Is there a parallel in modern America with the class warfare which was so common in Rome? Explain.

B. Do you think exchanging the oligarchy for the type of rule promised by Catiline would have benefited the majority of people? Why?

CHAPTER III

Early Stages of the Conspiracy
(25-33)

1. What did Catiline need to do before he joined his army in war in Rome?

2. What was the "last decree of the Senate?"

3. What was the mood in Rome when the plot was uncovered?

4. What did the conspirators claim was their reason for fighting?

5. What did Catiline claim to be doing?

Chapter IV

Party Strife at Rome
(36-40)
1. What did Sallust claim about the supporters of the conspiracy?

2. What did he say about the tribunes?

Chapter V

The Betrayal of the Conspiracy
(42-49)
1. How did Cicero find out about the plot?

2. What dilemma did Cicero face when the conspirators were caught?

3. What were the Sibylline Books?

4. Once the plot was uncovered, how did the common people respond?

5. Two rivals of Caesar, Catulus and Piso, sought to have others lie about him. Why?

Chapter VI

The Debate in the Senate and the Punishment of the Conspirators
(50-55)
1. What did Caesar say about emotions of hatred, affection, anger and compassion?

2. What did he say about freedom of individuals to show resentment?

3. According to Caesar, then, why would a harsh punishment for the conspirators be wrong?

4. What was the *lex porcia*?

5. Why did Caesar caution against too harsh a punishment?

6. What were some of the practices or materials which Rome adopted from others?

Unit 2: History

7. What did Caesar propose for the conspirators?

8. According to Cato, what was at stake for Rome?

9. What did he abhor?

10. According to Cato, how had the use of language been changed?

11. What did Cato believe about Caesar?

12. What did Cato say about the founders of the Republic?

13. What did Cato propose?

14. How did Sallust describe Caesar and Cato?

15. What did the senate decide to do?

Question for Further Thought

Can you give examples of euphemisms which are commonly used today?

Words to Know

profligate:

incendiarism:

euphemism:

impecunious:

repartee:

coup d'etat:

indolent:

Chapter VII

Defeat and Death of Catiline
(58-61)

1. When Catiline's army received word that the Roman conspirators had been executed, what did they do?

2. What problem did Catiline have as he marched toward Gaul?

3. What were the Romans told they were defending?

4. How did Catiline's troops fight?

5. What was the result?

The Conspiracy of Catiline

About Cicero and His Work

Cicero, also known as Tully, was born in 106 B.C. in Arpinum, into the class known as Knights. He moved to Rome when he was fourteen years old and had the best tutors. He excelled in literature, rhetoric, law and philosophy. Cicero became known through the many speeches he delivered in the senate and courts of law.

Cicero rose through the ranks of Roman government and ran for consul. He was at a disadvantage in seeking office because he did not have the ancestry which was usually a prerequisite for the job, but due to the fact that his rival was Catiline, who was rumored to be a revolutionary, he was elected in 64 B.C. During the second half of his consulship he was successful in prosecuting Catiline who was leading a conspiracy of uprisings, and he joined with conservatives against agrarian reforms. Unfortunately for Cicero, he was too jubilant about his success in defeating Catiline and public opinion turned against him. In 59 B.C., Caesar wanted Cicero to be part of the *Triumvirate* with himself and Pompey, but Cicero did not like Caesar's unconstitutional stand, and he refused. Clodius, who detested him, brought charges against Cicero for executing citizens without trial, and he was banished from Rome. His family was persecuted and his house was demolished.

He was recalled to Rome and civic duties a couple of years later, with the consent of Caesar. During the civil war between Caesar and Pompey in 50 B.C., he sided with Pompey. Caesar sought to squelch the activity of the senate and other republican institutions, and Pompey opposed him. Pompey lost. Cicero believed that dictatorial rule was wrong because it curtailed individual freedom. Ultimate authority should be based on moral principles which were not subject to personal whims. Rome entered her last days of the Republic, was ruled by mobs, and the provinces were plundered.

Cicero preferred being remembered as a philosopher, not an orator. His contributions to literature and thought are undisputed. He perfected Latin prose and his work became the basis of literary expression in Renaissance Europe. Students of Latin always read some of his carefully crafted essays. His ideas influenced the thought of St. Jerome, St. Ambrose, St. Augustine, Petrarch, Erasmus, Roger Bacon and many others.

Cicero delivered 14 speeches, known as the *Philippics*, against Antony, and when Antony and Octavius came to power in 43 B.C., he was killed.

Attack on an Enemy of Freedom

by Cicero
Translation: Michael Grant
Penguin Classics

Cicero wrote this essay after the death of Caesar. The Republic was not to be restored and Antony grasped at dictatorial power. Brutus and Cassius had left Rome, and Antony gathered armed supporters and claimed land in Gaul for five years, through a law he created. Cicero returned from his travels to Greece and delivered his first *Philippic* to the senate. *Philippics* were speeches given by Cicero in imitation of speeches given by Demosthenes in the fourth century against King Philip II of Macedon. There were fourteen such speeches and this was the second. This second *Philippic* was never delivered publicly, but was distributed as a political pamphlet. After writing twelve additional *Philippics*, Antony and Octavian had Cicero murdered.

Unit 2: History

(I,1-II,3)
1. What does Cicero say about his enemies?

2. Why did he have so many enemies?

3. What "favor" had Antony done for Cicero?

4. What did Cicero accuse Antony of doing?

(V,11-IX,20)
5. What brought death to Clodius and Curio and now threatened Antony?

6. Why did Antony disapprove of Cicero's consulship?

7. What did Antony accuse Cicero of doing?

(XI,25-XII,28)
8. How do we know that Cicero thought the murder of Caesar was good?

9. What inconsistency does Cicero see?

10. What does Cicero say to the assumption that he is an accomplice?

(XIV,34-XV,39)
11. Whom does Cicero say benefited most from Caesar's death and how?

12. How did Antony "inherit" so much property?

13. Why did Antony not inherit his own father's property?

(XXI,53-XXVI,64)
14. What became of Pompey, former consuls, praetors, tribunes and most of the senate under Caesar?

15. To whom does Cicero compare Antony and why?

16. How did Antony travel around Italy?

17. What was done with Pompey's property when Caesar returned from Alexandria?

18. What does the following mean in this context: "Ill-gotten gains will soon be squandered?"

Words to Know

effrontery:

auspices:

fatuity:

parricide:

quaestor:

Attack on an Enemy of Freedom

19. How long did it take Antony to squander Pompey's property?

(XXX,75-XXXV,88)
20. What solecism did Antony commit as Master of the Horse?

21. What epithet does Cicero give Antony?

22. What did Antony offer Caesar at the Lupercalian feast?

23. Did Caesar accept it?

24. What is the significance of a diadem?

25. What happened on the fifteenth (the ides) of March?

26. What did Antony do at Caesar's funeral?

27. What did Antony do after Caesar's funeral which seemed promising for Rome?

28. What did he then do which would prove disastrous for Rome?

(XLIII,111-XLV,116)
29. What is a man's best protection in a place such as Rome, according to Cicero?

30. What does Cicero say about the kind of man Caesar was?

31. What warning does Cicero give Antony?

32. What two things does Cicero desire?

Words to Know

solecism:

lachrymose:

Master of the Horse:

libel:

slander:

Unit 2: History

Questions for Further Thought

A. Judging from this portrayal of Antony, was there any reason the people of Rome could have wanted him as a leader?

B. Could a person get away with distributing a pamphlet written in this manner today?

Attack on Misgovernment

by Cicero
Translation: Michael Grant
Penguin Classics

"Against Verres"

(Introduction)
1. Who was Verres?

2. What was he accused of?

3. What had Sulla done to change the composition of the court?

(I,1-V,13)
4. What did Cicero say about the court as he began to speak?

5. What had Verres done?

6. How did Cicero feel in the court?

7. Why did Cicero refrain from giving details of Verres' lust?

(VII,18-XIII,39)
8. What did Curio proclaim to Verres?

9. How had Verres attempted to keep Cicero out of the office of *aedile*?

10. Why does Cicero say he took the case?

11. What did he hope to accomplish?

12. How did the people view the court?

(XV,44-XVII,52)
13. What two characteristics did Cicero attribute to Verres?

14. What happened to Verres?

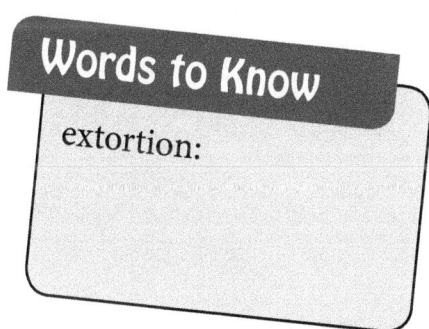

Words to Know

extortion:

Unit 2: History

The Annals of Imperial Rome

by Tacitus
Translation: Michael Grant
Penguin Classics

Much of what we know about Tacitus is gleaned from his own writings, *The Annals* and *The Histories*, and from letters written to him by his friend Pliny the Younger. He lived from 55 A.D. till 117 A.D. He studied rhetoric under Quintillian during the reign of Vespasian, and he excelled in the skill. He married the daughter of the Governor of Britain, Julius Agricola, and served various emperors in the positions of *quaestor*, *aedile* and *praetor*.*

Tacitus served his country away from Rome for a number of years, and when he returned the tyranny of Domitian was well established. To test the loyalty of his senate, Domitian demanded full attendance when honorable men were murdered, and he demanded flattery as well. Informants recorded reactions, and people lived in fear. Domitian was assassinated in 96 and the tyranny ended.

Tacitus vowed to maintain the memory of those terrible times as well as to witness to the happiness of the present time. His works were released during the reign of Trajan. He became consul in 97 and was proconsul of Asia.

Note to the reader: I have put both book and chapter headings because different editions of *The Annals* are annotated using one or the other way. Thus, the numbers will follow the book numbers which are consistent through the various editions.

---

* *quaestor*: elected official in charge of the state treasury

  aedile: magistrate in charge of temples, buildings, markets and games; preserved the decrees of the people; later in charge of the corn supply

  praetor: title of the magistrate who administered justice between Roman citizens; some governed provinces, and all were elected annually by the people

Unit 2: History

Book I

Chapter 1
(A.D. 14) From Augustus to Tiberius
(1-4)
1. What does Tacitus say of previously written histories?
2. Who established freedom and the consulship in Rome?
3. During crises, was the government managed?
4. What does Tacitus state his purpose to be?
5. How did Augustus win people over?
6. Who was the treacherous wife of Augustus and the mother of Tiberius?
7. How does Tacitus describe the state?

(5-14)
8. Who succeeded Augustus?
9. What was the first crime of the new reign?
10. What was the first order of business?
11. What does Tacitus say about the peace of Augustus?
12. What happened to men whom Augustus thought would be able leaders?
13. How did Tiberius feel about honor paid to Augusta (his mother)

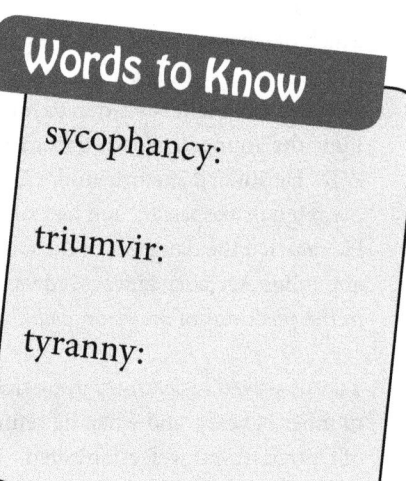

Words to Know

sycophancy:

triumvir:

tyranny:

Chapter 2
Mutiny on the Frontiers
(26-31)
1. What were some of the soldiers' demands in the meeting at Pannonia?
2. How might the moon's going dark at this time be explained?
3. How was order restored to the mob?

4. What did Drusus (the emperor's son) promise the soldiers?

5. Where else was mutiny threatened? Who was in charge there?

(32-37)
6. What characterized this mutiny?

7. Who was Germanicus?

8. What troubled him?

9. How was Germanicus different from Tiberius?

10. Who had the people of Rome wanted as their emperor?

11. What did Germanicus do when the soldiers said they would support him if he wanted to be emperor?

12. How was the mutiny resolved?

(40-44)
13. Why were the people indignant?

14. How did Germanicus respond?

15. When he addressed the troops, what did he say?

16. What was done to the leaders?

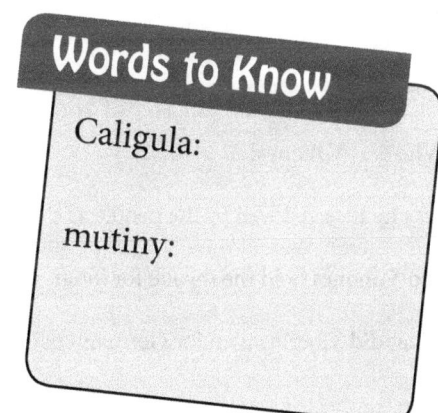

Words to Know

Caligula:

mutiny:

CHAPTER 3
(A.D. 14 and 15) War with the Germans
(51-55)
1. How did the soldiers expiate their guilt for the mutiny?

2. What two German generals divided the German people?

3. Which one allied himself with Rome?

4. What did Arminius do?

(60-69)
5. As Germanicus marched, what did he come upon near the forest of Teotoburgium?

Unit 2: History

6. What did Germanicus do?

7. Who prevented the bridge over the Rhine from being destroyed?

8. What did Tiberius think of Agrippina?

9. What had Agrippina done that the emperor could not?

(72-81)
10. What law was revived during Tiberius' second year as emperor?

11. What was going on in the theaters during this time?

12. What does Tacitus say about elections under Tiberius?

Words to Know

sinecure:

parapet:

BOOK II

(A.D. 16-19)
(1-5)
1. Who was Vonones?

2. Was he received well by the people as their king?

3. Did Vonones hold the throne for long?

4. What did Tiberius plan for Germanicus?

(14-23)
5. What happened the night before Germanicus took on the Germans under Arminius?

6. What was the result of the battle with the Germans?

7. What happened as Germanicus was returning to Italy?

(24-26)
8. What did Tiberius want Germanicus to do?

9. What did Germanicus want instead?

10. How did Tiberius respond to Germanicus' request for another year?

Chapter 4
(A.D. 16 and 17) The First Treason Trials
(38-51)
1. How did Tiberius respond to Hortalus' request for money from the government?

2. How did Tiberius get Germanicus out of Rome?

3. What was the relationship between Germanicus and Drusus like?

4. How was Appuleria punished for adultery?

5. How did Tiberius feel about strife in the senate between his sons Germanicus and Drusus and the law regarding the appointment of a *praetor*?

Chapter 5
(A.D. 18-20) The Death of Germanicus
(54-55)
1. What did the priest at Colophon predict for Germanicus?

2. How did Germanicus' decency manifest itself with regard to Piso?

3. How did Piso repay Germanicus?

4. Why didn't Germanicus do something about it?

(59-71)
5. How did Germanicus imitate Scipio when he went to Egypt?

6. When Germanicus became sick, what was thought to be the cause?

7. What did Germanicus say as he was dying?

(73-End of Chapter)
8. How was Germanicus compared to Alexander the Great?

9. How was Germanicus unlike Alexander the Great?

Unit 2: History

Book III

(A.D. 20-22)
(1-5)
1. What did Agrippina carry as she disembarked at Corcyra?

2. Who were conspicuously absent from the funeral?

3. Where was the final resting place for the ashes?

4. How was Agrippina perceived by the Romans?

5. What was absent from the honors due Germanicus as compared to honors previously given to comparable dignitaries?

(6-13)
6. What excuse did Tiberius give for not providing those honors?

7. When Drusus went to Piso in Syria, what did he say?

8. What were the charges against Piso?

(14-18)
9. Which of the charges could not be proven?

10. What did the people do while waiting for a verdict?

11. What was Tiberius' demeanor through the trial?

12. What happened the night Piso was to prepare his own defense?

13. Why was Plancina acquitted?

14. What does Tacitus say about history?

The Annals of Imperial Rome

 Questions for Further Thought

A. How would you characterize Tiberius?

B. What kinds of hints has Tacitus given that he did not admire Tiberius?

Chapter 6
(A.D. 20 - 22) Tiberius and the Senate
(24-26)
1. What misfortunes did Augustus have at home?

2. What was the *Papia Poppaea* Law?

3. Why did the law fail to increase the number of marriages and children?

4. How would you summarize Tacitus' view of mankind?

(28-34)
5. What does Tacitus say about the constitution of Caesar Augustus?

6. Who does Tacitus say relieved some of the problems of those laws?

7. What excuses did Sevirus Caecina give for magistrates not taking wives to the provinces?

8. How did Valerius Messalinus respond?

(52-65)
9. Legislation against what was undertaken under Casius Sulpicius and Didius Haterius?

10. What were the questions which concerned Tiberius?

11. What had changed in Rome to make men greedy?

12. Where did Tacitus say the solution lay?

13. What does Tacitus say is the function of history?

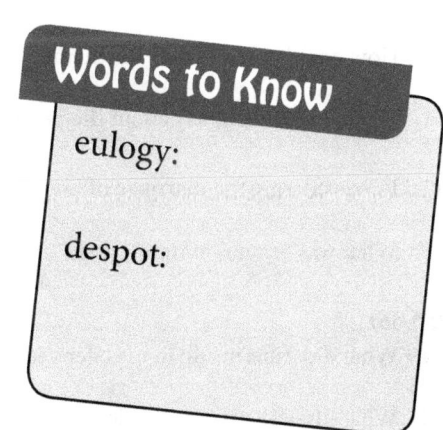

Words to Know

eulogy:

despot:

Unit 2: History

14. What was Tiberius known to say whenever he left the senate after witnessing the foolish legislation proposed by the senators?

Book IV

Chapter 7
(A.D. 23-29) Partner of my Labours
(1-3)
1. How did Tiberius view Germanicus' death?

2. To what does Tacitus attribute Tiberius' change in behavior?

3. Who was Sejanus?

4. How did Sejanus get vengeance on Drusus after a fight?

(8-12)
5. What was the cause of Drusus' illness?

6. After Drusus died, to whom did Tiberius entrust Germanicus' sons Nero and Drusus?

7. Why didn't the Roman people mourn the death of Drusus?

(17-30)
8. After Drusus was out of the way, whom did Sejanus target next?

9. What does Tacitus say about informers?

(32-41)
10. How does Tacitus restate his theme?

11. What does Tacitus say about the persecution of genius?

12. In considering the marriage of Livia and Sejanus, what did Tiberius say had to regulate his actions?

13. What was Sejanus' ultimate goal?

(56-66)
14. What did Tiberius do in his later years?

15. What disaster occurred which was the result of shoddy construction?

16. What did the leading Roman citizens do which was the practice of their ancestors after a disaster?

17. How did Tiberius spend his time away from Rome?

Book V

(A.D. 29-31)
(2-5)
1. What effect did Tiberius' mother, the Augusta, have while she lived?

2. What happened after she died?

3. What is lost from *The Annals*?

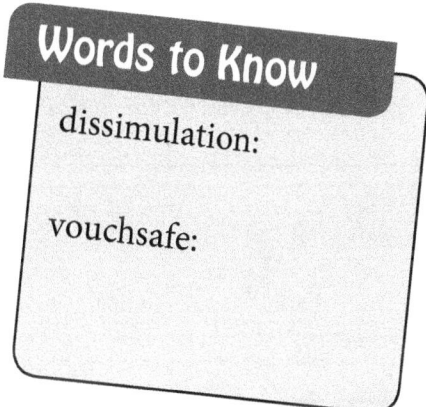

Words to Know

dissimulation:

vouchsafe:

Book VI

Chapter 8
(A.D. 32-37) The Reign of Terror
(4-8)
1. What did Tacitus say about the souls of despots?

2. During this time when everybody was distancing himself from Sejanus, Marcus Terentius admitted to being his friend. What were his reasons?

(9-20)
3. During this period when Tiberius was "cleaning house" few people of prominence died natural deaths. Tacitus gives an example even of an old woman who was executed. What was her crime?

4. What was the result of wide-spread brutality?

5. What two views of fate and chance does Tacitus discuss?

(24-28)
6. What did Tiberius accuse Agrippina of?

7. What happened to her?

8. Why did Nerva choose to die?

Unit 2: History

9. Why did so many in Rome commit suicide?

(45-51)
10. How did Tiberius turn the fire in Rome to his own glory?

11. What was Tiberius' concern in bequeathing the empire?

12. What were the events leading up to Tiberius' death?

13. How did Tacitus summarize the life of Tiberius?

Words to Know

importunate:

sycophant:

Question for Further Thought

Did Tiberius' death befit that of an emperor of the most powerful state in the Western World at the time?

The four years of the reign of Caligula and the first six years of the reign of his uncle Claudius, are lost.

Book XI

Chapter 9
(A.D. 47-48) The Fall of Messalina
(1-12)
1. Who was Messalina?

2. What kind of person was she?

3. Who was Nero?

4. What were some of Claudius' accomplishments?

(24-26)
5. What did Claudius say was the ruin of Sparta and Athens?

6. How did Claudius propose to rid the senate of undesirables?

7. What did Messalina's lover, Gaius Silius, say about flagrant guilt?

8. What did he propose?

9. What did Messalina do as soon as Claudius left Rome for Ostia?

(30-38)
10. How did Claudius respond to charges that his wife was engaged in intrigue?

11. What did Claudius plan?

12. What did Claudius ask Messalina to do?

13. What happened to her?

14. Who was Narcissus?

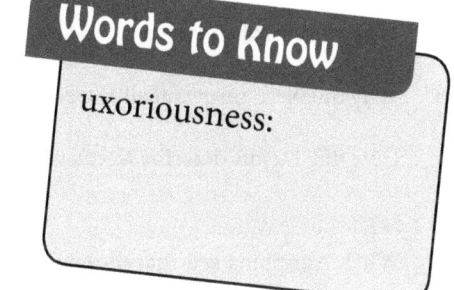

uxoriousness:

Book XII

Chapter 10
(A.D. 48-54) The Mother of Nero
(3-8)
1. Who was chosen as a wife for Claudius?

2. How did the people come to accept the incestuous marriage of Claudius and Agrippina?

3. What did Agrippina do to counter the opinion that she only engaged in bad actions?

(19-22)
4. When Mithridates sued for peace after having been defeated, what did he ask?

5. Why did Claudius agree?

6. In what treachery did Agrippina involve herself?

(25-69)
7. Why was Domitius adopted by Claudius?

8. What name was Domitius given?

9. How did Claudius die?

Unit 2: History

Book XIII

Chapter 11
(A.D. 54-58) The Fall of Agrippina
(1-10)
1. Who was the first to die by treachery during the reign of Nero?

2. Who were Africanus Burrus and Annaeus Seneca?

3. Why did Nero throw off all respect for his mother?

4. How did Tacitus describe Nero's wife Octavia?

(14-25)
5. When Agrippina saw that she could not influence Nero any longer, what did she call for?

6. What happened to the fourteen-year-old Britannicus?

7. What did Tacitus say is the most precarious and transitory human thing?

8. What did Nero do in the disguise of a slave?

Book XIV

(A.D. 59-62)
(1-5)
1. Agrippina was immoral to the core. What final act led to Nero's decision to kill her?

2. How did Anicetus suggest Agrippina be killed?

3. What happened the night the plan was carried out?

(8-11)
4. What finally happened to Agrippina?

5. What had the astrologers predicted many years before?

6. What did Nero do after his mother's death to justify what had happened?

Words to Know

impunity:

dissipation:

truncheon:

Chapter 12
Nero and his Helpers
(14-21)

1. What two amusements did Nero especially like?

2. Which amusement was indulged by Seneca and Burrus?

3. What went on during the "youth games?"

4. What did a comet signify to the Romans?

(35-59)

5. What was unusual about the Britons in war?

6. After Burrus died, Seneca's position put him in danger. What did he request from the emperor?

7. How did Nero respond to his request?

8. Why did Nero hate his wife Octavia?

9. What happened after Nero divorced Octavia and married his mistress Poppea?

QUESTION FOR FURTHER THOUGHT

Why did Octavia hide her emotions about the death of her brother Britannicus?

BOOK XV

Chapter 13
(A.D. 62-65) Eastern Settlement
(1-6)

1. Who said that "passivity does not preserve great empires; that needs fighting, with warriors and weapons. When stakes are highest, might is right. A private individual can satisfy his prestige by holding his own - but a monarch can only do it by claiming other people's property."

2. Why was the war suspended between Vologeses and Corbulo?

Unit 2: History

(14-18)
3. What honor did Vologeses say had been granted the Arasids by heaven?

4. What was agreed to by Vologeses and Corbulo?

5. Despite the outcome of the Parthian War, what did Nero do?

Chapter 14
The Burning of Rome
(32-36)
1. In addition to the excessive gladiatorial displays, what else could be witnessed in Rome?

2. Where did Nero choose to make his public debut on the stage?

3. Why did the people of Rome want Nero to stay in Rome rather than travel to distant places?

(38-43)
4. According to Tacitus, what preceded the burning of Rome?

5. What was the layout of Rome at the time?

6. Where was Nero rumored to be when Rome burned?

7. How was Rome rebuilt?

(44-end of Chapter)
8. On whom did Nero place the blame for the fire?

9. Why did he blame them?

10. What was done to the Christians?

11. How did Tacitus describe the Christians?

12. What did the people think of Nero's actions?

Question for Further Thought

What does this account from Tactitus about the Christians collaborate?

The Annals of Imperial Rome

Chapter 15
The Plot
(50-57)

1. What did the conspirators against Nero plan?

2. Why did Piso refuse to allow Nero to be murdered in his home?

3. Why did the plot fail?

4. What weakness did the knights and senators involved in the conspiracy show?

desultory:

styptic:

incendiary:

(59-67)

5. What became of Piso?

6. How did Seneca respond to the announcement of his death sentence?

7. How did Subrius Flavus respond to Nero's question of why he had conspired against him?

8. What happened to Subrius?

Question for Further Thought

Tacitus says that the deaths of Claudius Senecio, Afranius Quintanius and Flavius Scavinus belied their effeminate lives. What does he mean?

Book XVI

Chapter 16
(A.D. 65-66) Innocent Victims
(4-16)

1. What was required of people who had to attend the spectacles in the theaters where Nero performed?

2. How did Poppaea die?

Unit 2: History

3. How does Tacitus describe the countless deaths and all the bloodshed?

4. To what does Tacitus ascribe this tragedy?

5. Why does Tacitus detail the deaths?

(22-35)
6. What "crimes" had Thrasea committed which merited the wrath of Nero?

7. What was Thrasea doing when he was awaiting death in his garden?

8. As he died, what did Thrasea say to the *quaestor*?

Words to Know

panegyric:

dichotomy:

intestate:

Questions for Further Thought

A. What did Tacitus think of the emperors of Rome?

B. Would Tacitus argue for the Republic or the Empire?

C. What were some of the virtues of those people who were noted by Tacitus to be free of corruption?

Drama
Unit Three

Roman Drama

Drama, as no other literary form, has the ability to touch the hearts or funny-bones of people, because it most often deals with universal human themes and gives a glimpse at ordinary life. While the Greeks had a highly developed form of drama, both tragedy and comedy nearly 500 years before the birth of Christ, the Romans did not create their own until their contact with the Greeks became more extensive in the third century B.C. The year 240 B.C. marks the beginning of Roman literature with the translation by a Greek slave/actor of a Greek comedy and a Greek tragedy into Latin.

The oldest piece of Roman literature is a collection of comedies, according to Edith Hamilton in her book *The Roman Way*. The Romans were not original in their creation of drama; rather they borrowed from what is known as the *New Greek Comedy* of the third century before Christ, not long after the First Punic War. Much of what we know about Roman life outside of the government and war machine is from these first comedies.

In Rome as in Greece, the plays were presented often in the context of religious celebrations. In Rome, the occasions were regularly scheduled games, temple dedications, festivals or funerals. It is estimated that in 200 B.C. five to eleven days were dedicated to such activity every year and by the time of Augustus, more than 40 days were so spent.

The Roman stage was long and narrow and designed to look like a city street. Buildings were simple and represented houses. Actors entered and existed on both ends of the stage and through the doors of the houses called *ostia* which faced the street. Actors exiting to the left were headed to the harbor and foreign destinations, and those exiting on the right were headed for the forum or other parts of the country. Sometimes there was a narrow street which crossed the main street and which ran between the houses. This was known as an *angiportum* and provided another exit to the forum or country. It was also a good place for the actor to listen in on the conversations of others.

Roman actors dressed like Greeks. They wore a *pallium* which was an outer garment worn over a long-sleeved tunic. Old men wore white and younger men wore red or purple. Slaves wore tunics and a scarf around their necks. Since all the actors were male, they wore long gowns with wigs when they played the part of women. Slaves were identified by red wigs. Experts have not concluded for sure whether or not Roman actors wore masks as the Greeks did.

The action of a Roman play was unbroken, except for short pauses in which there may have been music played on a flute. Song and dance were

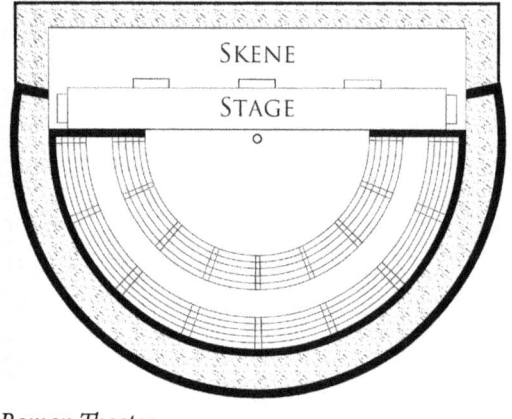

Roman Theater

integrated into the plays and were thought to be perfected by Plautus. As actors entered and exited the stage, they often announced where they were going or where they had been. The plays often opened with a *monologue* which set the scene, while other literary devises used were *asides* and *soliloquies* which revealed the thoughts of the actor. Slaves were often portrayed running about the stage and delivering monologues.

Tragedy was never developed to the extent that it was in Greece. Much of the tragedy that was written was adapted from Greek themes, and Seneca was the primary tragic writer. The two comedy writers who stand out in Rome are Plautus and Terence. In this work we will look at *The Brothers Menaechmi* by Plautus, and *The Brothers* by Terence.

Much of the information for this introduction is from *The Complete Roman Drama,* edited by George E. Duckworth.

Unit 2: History

The Brothers Menaechmi

by Plautus
Translation: E. F. Watling
Penguin Classics

Little is known about Plautus, who lived from 254 to 184 B.C. He is remembered as the leading writer of comedy from ancient Rome. He wrote over 40 plays but only 20 survive in their entirety. Plautus imitated Greek comedy in form, but his characters were Latin and his settings and characters were Italian. His work was slapstick in nature and loved by the Roman public. It was imitated down through the ages by such people as Shakespeare, Moliere and Ben Johnson.

Plautus used song and dance in addition to dialogue in his plays. This was a break from the tradition of drama which he copied from the Greeks. The result was a lively musical farce. The themes were often predictable and included thwarted love, mistaken identity, intrigue and trickery. By using Greek names and settings, Plautus was able to avoid the laws which forbade the lampooning of public officials.

Plautus wrote in the language of the people, not in formal Latin. His work is replete with puns and humorous made-up words. He portrayed vice as repulsive and virtue as something to be rewarded. To make his plays Roman, he included references to Roman places, people and events.

The divisions into Acts is not in the original work, but is inserted to give the reader a sense of structure. The plays were presented as a whole and the scenes changed merely by moving from one part of the stage to another.

The Brothers Menaechmi

The Brothers Menaechmi is a comedy of errors, and it has the standard elements of farce, deception, mistaken identity and plotting which were found in Roman comedy. It influenced Shakespeare to write *A Comedy of Errors* many centuries later.

Unit 3: Drama

Prologue

1. What is the setting of the play?
2. Who is speaking?
3. Where do the comic writers claim to set their plays?
4. In truth, where does this play take place?
5. What story does the unknown speaker tell?

Act I

1. What does the name Peniculus mean?
2. What is the most effective way to keep a slave or prisoner from running away?
3. Why is Peniculus going to see Menaechmus?
4. Who is Menaechmus yelling at and why?
5. Where is Menaechmus headed?
6. According to Peniculus, who is being punished?
7. What has Menaechmus done?
8. What does Menaechmus promise Peniculus?
9. What does Menaechmus propose to Erotium?

Act II

1. Who is Sosicles?
2. Why has Menaechmus 2 come to Epidamnus?
3. How long has he been searching?
4. What happens outside of Erotium's house?

The Brothers Menaechmi

5. Why does Cylindrus refer to Menaechmus 2's companion as "fellow-guests?"

6. What does Menaechmus 2 offer Cylindrus?

7. How does Messenio explain Cylindrus' knowledge of Menaechmus 2's name?

8. Whom does Erotium see outside her house?

9. What does Erotium say that reveals her true intentions?

10. How does Erotium convince Menaechmus 2 to enter her house?

11. What does Erotium ask Menaechmus 2 to do with the dress Menaechmus brought her?

ACT III

1. Why did Peniculus miss his lunch?

2. What does Peniculus hear Menaechmus 2 telling Erotium?

3. What happens when Peniculus meets Menaechmus 2?

4. What does Peniculus threaten to do when Menaechmus 2 says he does not know him and sees him with the dress?

5. What happens after Peniculus enters the house?

6. What kind of work does Menaechmus do?

7. What matters most to him about his clients?

8. What does his wife hear him say?

9. What does Menaechmus claim to have done with the dress?

10. What does his wife tell him?

11. What does Menaechmus ask of Erotium?

12. How does she respond?

Unit 3: Drama

Act IV

1. Whom does the wife see coming down the street?
2. What does she tell him when he doesn't acknowledge that the dress is hers?
3. How does her father respond to her complaints?
4. Under what circumstance would her father plead for her against her husband?
5. Why should she be satisfied with him?
6. What does Menaechmus 2 pretend?
7. Whom does Menaechmus 2 pretend to be obeying?
8. After Menaechmus 2 falls to the ground, where does the father go?
9. What does Menaechmus 2 do?

Act V

1. Whom do the father and the doctor meet on the street?
2. What does the doctor tell the father to do?
3. What is Menaechmus' predicament?
4. What does Messenio say about how a slave behaves?
5. What does Messenio witness?
6. What does Messenio request?
7. Where does Messenio go?
8. Whom does Messenio meet on his way to the inn?
9. What does Messenio see?
10. What does he tell his master, Menaechmus 2?

11. Who solves the case?

12. After the brothers realize they are twins, what does Menaechmus decide to do?

13. Who will be the auctioneer?

Questions for Further Thought

   A. What does this play say about Roman lawyers?

   B. What does the play say about Roman morality?

Unit 3: Drama

The Brothers
(Adelphi)

by Terence
Translation: Robert Graves
Aldine Publishing

Terence was born a slave after the Second Punic War in Carthage around 195 B.C. He was taken to Rome and sold to a Roman senator who raised him as a patrician. He took his master's name and had as a *cognomen* Afer, which referred to his birthplace; thus his name was Publius Terentius Afer. His polished qualities were noticed by the son of Scipio Africanus, and he enjoyed the patronage and company of his circle of friends.

When Terence was around 34 years of age he went to Greece and on becoming familiar with the work of Menander, translated 108 of his comedies. This experience led him to write his own works, six of which still exist.

While Terence was a comedy writer, his work was refined and not burlesque as had been the work of Plautus. He introduced suspense by eliminating an explanatory prologue and his endings caught the audience by surprise. He sometimes merged the plots of more than one Greek play, and that caused not a little uproar. Nevertheless, his work appealed to the more educated classes and left him with the reputation as one of the two great Roman comedy writers.

The Brothers

The introduction to the play says that it was:

A comedy performed at the Funeral Games of L. Aemilius Paulus when Q. Fabius Maximus and P. Cornelius Africanus were Curule Ediles. The music, performed on Tyrian flutes, was composed by a freedman of Claudius named Flaccus. It was taken from the Greek of Menander and performed during the Consulship of L. Ancinius and M. Cornelius. 160 B.C.

Unit 3: Drama

Prologue

1. Where does the play take place?

2. How does Micio set the tone of the play in the opening scene?

Act I

1. Who is Aeschinus?

2. How does Micio parent?

3. What does Micio say is a father's function?

4. What has Aeschinus done?

5. Who is Ctesipho and what does his father Demea say about him?

6. What is Micio's reaction to what his son has done?

7. What excuse does Micio give for not having behaved like Aeschinus when he was young?

8. What does Micio advise his brother?

9. How does Micio really feel?

Act II

1. What has Aeschinus done?

2. Who is Sannio?

3. Why did Aeschinus kidnap the girl?

Act III

1. Why is Geta upset?

2. What dilemma does the family face?

3. What does Sostrata propose?

4. What does Syrus mean when he says "as each man wants his son to be, so the son appears to his father?"

5. What lie does Syrus tell Demea?

6. What is the play poking fun at?

7. What crime has Aeschinus committed?

ACT IV

1. How does Syrus propose to placate Demea?

2. What story does Syrus tell Demea?

3. What story will Hegio tell Sostrata?

4. What does Micio tell Aeschinus about what he has done to Pamphila?

5. Whom does Demea tell Micio Aeschinus has debauched?

6. What is Micio's attitude toward the problem?

7. What does Micio say he will do with the music-girl?

ACT V

1. What is Demea's main concern for Aeschinus and Ctesipho, money or morals?

2. What does Demea say after he agrees to take the girl back to the country with Ctesipho?

3. How old is Micio?

4. What does Demea do?

5. What does Demea say in response to Micio's question as to why he has changed?

Unit 3: Drama

Questions for Further Thought

A. What does Demea mean when he says he has stabbed his brother with his own weapon?

B. Is Terence making a case for indulgence or restraint in this play?

C. What behaviors did Micio seem to dismiss as normal among Roman men which are not considered moral today?

Philosophy ~ Religion
Unit Four

Unit 4: Philosophy ~ Religion

Philosophy ~ Religion
Unit Four

Unit 4: Philosophy ~ Religion

Meditations

by Marcus Aurelius
Translation: Maxwell Staniforth
Penguin Classics

Marcus Annius Verus was born in 121 A.D. in Rome of Spanish parents who had settled there. His father died while Marcus was just an infant, so he was raised by his mother and paternal grandfather. From them he learned virtue and piety, and they saw to it that he learned Latin and Greek, literature, philosophy, art and painting. From his teacher, Diognetus the Stoic, he learned to desire Greek discipline, such as sleeping on a plank bed with an animal skin for cover. While a very young child he endeared himself to Hadrian who called him *Verissimus*, which means most sincere or true.

After Hadrian died, the title of Caesar was given to Marcus Aurelius in 139. In 140 he served as consul, and later he shared power with his adoptive brother Antonius Pius, who was the emperor. After Antonius died, Marcus shared power and title with his adopted brother Lucius Commodus, but his brother did not share the burdens of state with him, as his interests were in the direction of seeking pleasure.

Marcus Aurelius's reign was marked by calamities, including floods, famine, earthquakes, barbarians crossing the frontiers, riots and sedition. The Parthians drove out the Armenian king who was a friend of Rome, and Syria was attacked. The Goths were forcing movement of German tribes into the Roman provinces and Marcus was forced to be away from Rome most of the time.

The *Meditations* were apparently written for himself during his time away from Rome fighting the Germans. He returned finally to Rome in 176 in triumph and took the title of Germanicus Maximus.

Marcus was unsympathetic to the Christians, blaming them for a severe pestilence which his legions picked up while in Parthia. He led a persecution of them which was one of the last and most brutal. He ruled Rome for 28 years and died at the age of 59 in 180 A.D.

Meditations

The *Meditations* records the thoughts, stoic philosophy, and mind of Marcus Aurelius. The format is like that of many works on meditation, in that it is a collection of specific numbered thoughts, not a work of prose in the usual sense. It is an expression of gratitude, thoughts on life and death and advice on how to live. In the ancient times, philosophy provided the way to live a good life. That was not the province of religion as it is today. Morality had nothing to do with religion. Thus, this work is classified under Philosophy.

Unit 4: Philosophy ~ Religion

Book I

1. Whom does Marcus Aurelius first credit with teaching him many of the virtues?

2. What important virtues did his mother teach him?

3. From Apollonius, he learned freedom of will and undeviating steadiness in purpose. What did he learn with regard to reason?

4. What did he learn from Sextus?

5. What irony did Fronto teach him?

6. What did he learn about the care of the body?

7. What did Marcus Aurelius learn from his ruler/father about pride?

8. What did Marcus Aurelius attribute the good things he learned to?

Words to Know

casuistry:

plaudit:

Questions for Further Thought

A. Alexander the Platonist taught Marcus not to use the words "I am too busy." He reasoned that those words were used to avoid normal societal obligations. What is the lesson for us?

B. From reading about what he learned from his family and teachers and assuming he lived what he learned, how would you characterize Marcus Aurelius?

C. Can you list at least eight virtues which he learned which are also Christian virtues?

Book II

1. What does Marcus Aurelius say about the relationships among all men?

2. Where do all things come from?

3. How does he say every act should be done?

4. What does he say about bad acts?

5. What does he say about death?

6. What does he say about the gods?

7. What does "reverence for the daemon (divine spirit) within" consist of?

8. What is the only thing which one can be deprived of?

9. How does the soul do violence to itself?

10. What is the end of rational animals?

11. Where does man find the power to live righteously?

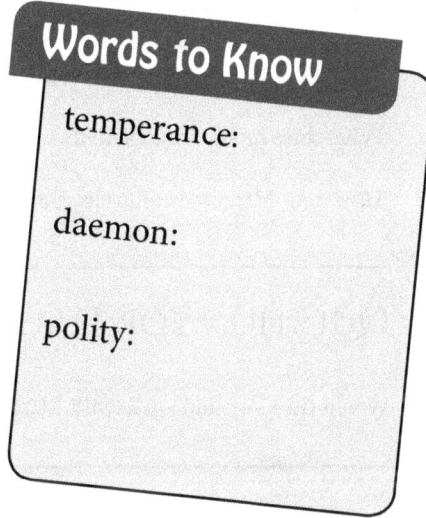

Words to Know

temperance:

daemon:

polity:

Book III

1. How should one react to things that happen?

2. Whose praise should a man not value?

3. What does Marcus mean when he says a man must stand erect, not be kept erect by others?

4. Marcus Aurelius says to avoid things profitable to oneself if they compel one to betray himself in what ways?

5. Marcus Aurelius, like the Greek philosophers before him, considers the body, the soul and the intelligence to be three parts of a whole, each with its own characteristics. What belongs to each?

6. How is the good man distinguished?

Book IV

1. What does Marcus Aurelius say about seeking retreat?

2. What does he say about the necessity of holding one's opinions?

Unit 4: Philosophy ~ Religion

3. What does he say about praise?

4. What does he say happens to souls?

5. What does he say about activity?

6. How does Marcus Aurelius look at life in the scheme of eternity?

Question for Further Thought

Would the Christian agree with Marcus Aurelius in seeing life as having little value?

Book V

1. How should one face each day?

2. What should one do after performing a good act?

3. To what does Marcus Aurelius attribute all things that happen?

4. How does man interfere with the integrity of the universe?

5. What does he say about harm to the state?

6. What does fortune mean?

Book VI

1. What is the best way for one to avenge himself?

2. What does Marcus Aurelius say about pretentiousness?

3. What is worthy of being valued?

4. What is the fruit of earthly life lived well?

5. How does Marcus Aurelius advise one to delight himself or use as a remedy for dejection?

6. When one encounters a hindrance in life, what should he do?

Book VII

1. How is the worth of a man figured?
2. What is necessary for anything to happen, i.e., nourishment, bathing, etc?
3. What is peculiar to man?
4. What duty do people have toward those who harm them?
5. How should we behave toward the things we have?
6. What does he say about Law?
7. What does he say that one learns about life by contemplating it?
8. What does he say about pain?

Question for Further Thought

What did Christ say about forgiving wrongdoers?

Book VIII

1. Why is it important to maintain an untroubled spirit?
2. How must one behave toward the foolish and ungrateful?
3. What is repentance?
4. Does Marcus Aurelius place value in pleasure?
5. What three relationships does everybody have?
6. What does Marcus Aurelius say about pain?

Unit 4: Philosophy ~ Religion

7. What power has God allowed to man alone?

8. If one is pained by an external thing, what causes the pain?

9. To what does Marcus Aurelius liken the mind that is free from passions?

10. What does he say about first appearances?

11. What does he say about wickedness?

Book IX

1. What does Marcus Aurelius name as sins?

2. What is the name of the universal Nature?

3. How should one view death?

4. From whom does death draw one away?

5. How does one sin?

6. From whom have we learned kindliness?

7. What should one do who has been blamed unjustly, or about whom something injurious has been said?

8. Does Marcus Aurelius value glory and the praises of others?

9. What should one pray for?

10. Why should one blame himself if offended by another's shameless conduct?

Question for Further Thought

In what frame of mind does Marcus Aurelius appear to be during the course of Book XI? Explain.

Book X

1. In order to be content with everything that happens, what does Marcus Aurelius say he must remember?

2. What does Marcus Aurelius advise about change?

3. When one is angry with another, what should he do?

4. What is common to all things?

5. What does Marcus Aurelius say all men have when dying?

6. In spite of that, what attitude should the dying have?

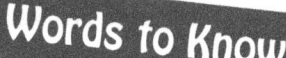

Words to Know

fatalism:

plaudit:

Questions for Further Thought

A. What does Marcus Aurelius say that illustrates the belief in fatalism?

B. What did Christ say about trying to removing the splinter from another's eye?

Book XI

1. What are the properties of a rational soul?

2. What was the purpose of stage tragedies?

3. What was the purpose of the old comedy?

4. How does one reveal his character?

5. What should one do when offended?

6. In contrast to being ruled by passion, what is manly behavior?

7. Marcus Aurelius gives a tenth rule to remember as a gift from Apollo. What is it?

Unit 4: Philosophy ~ Religion

Questions for Further Thought

A. Marcus Aurelius says that there is more virility in a man who is gentle and peaceable than in the one who is angry and discontented. Do you agree? Why, or why not?

B. What is the origin of the word virility and how do we understand it today?

Book XII

1. Does Marcus Aurelius believe in life beyond death?

2. What is a pugilist and why should one follow his example?

3. What three counsels does Marcus Aurelius give?

4. What does Marcus Aurelius say about man's intelligence?

5. How does Marcus Aurelius see the gods?

6. What or who determines the length of our days?

Questions for Further Thought

A. What are five beliefs that Marcus Aurelius appears to have had in common with Christians?

B. What are two differences in belief between his and the Christians?

C. How does Marcus Aurelius seem to differ from other emperors you have read about (i.e. Nero, Tiberius, etc)?

D. Do you think this work was written to counsel others, or was Marcus Aurelius trying to convince himself?

RESEARCH TOPIC:

Research the Stoic philosophy which came from Greece and how it was either accepted or rejected by the Romans. Who were the leading Stoics, and what key beliefs of Stoicism were reflected in the *Meditations* of Marcus Aurelius?

Unit 4: Philosophy ~ Religion

Selections from Early Christian Writings

Translation: Maxwell Staniforth
Penguin Classics

Early Christian Writings is a collection of the writings of a group of men known as the Apostolic Fathers, including Clement, Ignatius, Polycarp, Hermas and Papias. These men were in some way associated with the Apostles of Jesus Chirst, upon whom the foundation of Christianity was entrusted. They were faithful to the teachings of the Apostles and to the Tradition of the Church through the second century.

These writers were leaders in the early Church, and they were concerned about their followers. Their letters addressed issues of morality, heresy and problems which arose among the people. They reveal the wisdom of the early fathers and preserve the teachings of the Church from her earliest beginnings.

Unit 4: Philosophy ~ Religion

Clement of Rome

Clement of Rome (Clemens Romanus) was the third successor of Peter as the Bishop of Rome. He reigned from 90 to 100 A.D. His letter was written from the Church in Rome to the Church in Corinth in 96 A.D. The Church had recently suffered the persecution of Domitian.

1. What unexpected misfortune had the Church at Rome suffered?

2. How did Clement begin his letter?

3. What problems did he address?

4. What remedy did he propose?

5. Why was Lot rewarded?

6. Why was Rahab rewarded?

7. Why did Clement write about creation?

8. Why did he discuss resurrection?

9. What did Clement say about work?

10. What image did Clement use in exhorting the people to obey their leaders?

11. Who is the head of the body of believers?

12. What did he say about the liturgy?

13. According to the endnotes, what do we learn about the term "laic man?"

14. Clement spoke of the dispute during the time of Moses regarding the priesthood. Why?

15. What had been the consequence in Corinth for the disunity and rejection by the people of their clergy?

16. What did he ask those leading the dissension to do?

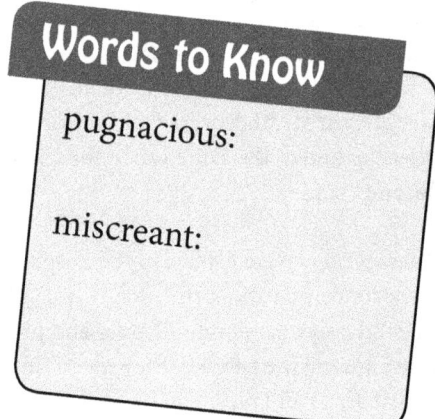

Words to Know

pugnacious:

miscreant:

Ignatius of Antioch, Bishop of Antioch, Syria

Ignatius of Antioch was martyred in 107 A.D. under Trajan, but we do not know for what reason specifically. He was taken in chains to Rome with a guard of 10 soldiers and feared that well-wishers would foil his ordered martyrdom. They went across the continent of Asia Minor and Northern Europe. In Smyrna, he was met by the leaders of some of the Southern Churches who went to bid him farewell. He gave each a letter to take back to his home church and also sent one to the Christians of Rome, his final destination.

He is honored for the theological teachings found in his letters as well as for the strong character he had exhibited as a martyr. After writing letters to the churches at Philadelphia, Smyrna and to Polycarp, the last thing recorded about Ignatius was his martyrdom in Rome on December 19, 107, and the removal of his bones back to Antioch.

The major heresy Ignatius taught against was Docetism. Docetists believed that material things, including the body, were worthless and impure. They thus taught that Christ, along with His life on earth, was only an illusion.

Letter to the Ephesians

Ephesus was the wealthy capital of the Roman province of Asia, and St. Paul had carried the Faith there. The Church had a good reputation but was being divided by Docetism. Ignatius was met on his way to Rome by a delegation led by Onesimus, and he gave him a letter to take back to his people.

The endnotes are instructive and should be read to further your understanding.

1. After greeting the Ephesians, what did Ignatius tell the people to do?

2. To what did he liken union with the bishop and clergy?

3. How did he admonish the people to regard the bishop?

4. What did he say the people should do with regard to those who "bandy the Name?"

5. How did he recommend the Ephesians deal with others?

6. How did he describe his chains?

7. What are the beginning and end of life?

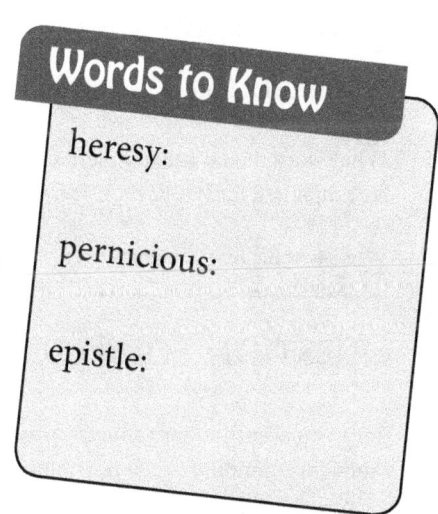

Words to Know

heresy:

pernicious:

epistle:

Unit 4: Philosophy ~ Religion

8. What was he speaking about when he discussed "defiling a household?"

9. According to the notes, what was a common attitude toward adultery?

10. What knowledge was kept from the devil, and how was it revealed?

11. How were the people to attend their meetings?

Question for Further Thought

Are any of the issues raised by Ignatius to the Ephesians relevant to Christians of today?

Letter to the Romans

Unlike his other letters, this one focuses on Ignatius' impending martyrdom rather than on admonitions against heresies and disobedience.

1. What did Ignatius fear?

2. What success had the Romans granted Peter and Paul?

3. In spite of what did Ignatius say Christianity achieved greatness?

4. What did he ask of the people?

5. What were his words in this regard?

6. What word did he use to describe the soldiers who accompanied him to Rome? Why?

7. What was his final request?

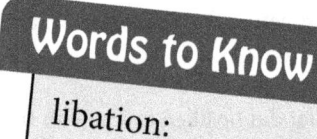

libation:

Question for Further Thought

Have you ever thought about the possibility of being martyred for your Faith? How do you see yourself responding to the possibility?

Polycarp of Smyrna (69-155 A.D.)

Polycarp was born in Asia, and that is where he spent his life. He was a disciple of St. John and, according to Irenaeus, was instructed by the Apostles. Smyrna was a center for pagan cults and Jews hostile to Christianity, so the young Christian Church struggled to survive. Internally the Church had to deal with schism and heresy.

Polycarp was bishop of Smyrna for half a century. Very little is recorded about his episcopate, but he was steadfast in his faith and taught what he believed. He was probably martyred in 155 during the proconsulship of Quadratus. As with many events of long ago, the exact date is difficult to ascertain.

The Martyrdom of Polycarp
by Marcion - an Eyewitness

1. To whom was this letter addressed?

2. To what did the writer attribute the endurance of the martyrs in the arena?

3. To whom did the Romans refer when they cried "Down with the infidels?"

4. What shame did Quintus commit?

5. How did Polycarp know the manner of his coming death?

6. What did Polycarp do when the police went to arrest him?

7. What was Polycarp's response to the governor when told to renounce Christ?

8. Why couldn't a lion be released to kill Polycarp?

9. What did the crowd call for?

10. How did the eyewitness describe what happened?

11. How did Polycarp die?

12. What happened?

13. What was done with his body?

14. How is the date of Polycarp's martyrdom described in the postscript?

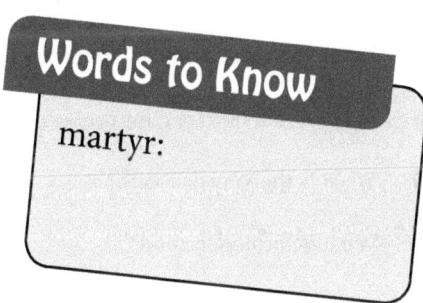

Words to Know

martyr:

Unit 4: Philosophy ~ Religion

Question for Further Thought

Without using the calendar date, can you describe the time of a certain historical event using eight descriptive phrases which would help historians find the calendar date?

The Didache

The Didache is the teaching of the Lord to the Gentiles through the twelve Apostles. It consists of two parts: an exposition of Christian morality and a collection of Church rules. It was a small volume of 120 leaves of parchment and was found in 1873. It had been written in Greek in 1056. The date of the original is disputed but the earliest Christian writers had referred to it, and it is likely no later than 150 A.D.

Part 1 - The Two Ways

1. What are the two ways?
2. What is the Way of Life?
3. What does the first part of the Commandment teach?
4. What does the second part of the Commandment proscribe?
5. What is meant in the *Didache* "do not equivocate in thought or speech?"
6. How should one behave toward bad men?
7. What virtues accompany meekness?
8. How should one treat his possessions?
9. What is the Way of Death?
10. What is forbidden food?

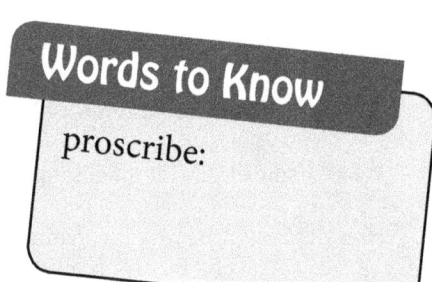

Words to Know

proscribe:

Part 2 - A Church Manual

1. What is prescribed for baptism?

2. What is said about fasting?

3. In the section "Of the Eucharist" what is covered?

4. In the section "Of Missioners and Charismatists" what instructions are given regarding them?

5. What is another name for charismatists and what did they do?

6. Who is to judge the veracity of the prophets?

7. Did the writer of the *Didache* give any clues as to how to discern if a prophet was genuine or not? If so, give examples.

8. How was Sunday to be observed?

9. What is the section "Eschatology" concerned with?

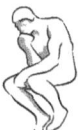

QUESTION FOR FURTHER THOUGHT

Does it matter how people in various places celebrate the rituals of the Faith? Why?

St. Augustine and His Works

St. Augustine was born November 13, 354, in Tagaste, Numidia Pro Consularis, a small town in Northern Africa near the eastern border of Algeria. Tagaste was a prosperous town under Rome.

Augustine and his family, though not rich, were associated with the Roman ruling class and the Christian community. His father was Patricius, a pagan and a minor official. His mother was Monica, a dedicated mother and a devout Catholic. His brother was named Navigus and his sister Perpetua entered religious life.

Augustine was a brilliant young man and was sent to study in Madauros which was a haven for paganism, and he was badly affected morally. He was later sent to Carthage to study rhetoric, and there his corruption was made complete. He took a concubine and had a son by her named Adeodatus (gift of God).

He became a Manichean. This heresy had the following elements:
- It was *gnostic*: it claimed to have special knowledge leading to salvation of a few, and in some of its forms denied the divinity of Christ
- It stressed extreme moral and metaphysical dualism
- Its sacred literature was more important than ritual
- It rejected the Old Testament entirely and attacked parts of the New Testament
- It saw the body as evil
- It claimed to appeal to reason
- It was a missionary religion, claiming to be universal.

Augustine's deficient moral and religious formation may have contributed to his embracing of the sect, but his great intellect and God's grace brought him not only to reject it but to become its greatest opponent.

Augustine became disillusioned with Manicheism and left secretly for Rome so that his mother would not follow him. There he opened a school of rhetoric but soon decided to leave for Milan where he received a post as Master of Rhetoric. His mother followed him there. Augustine was still under the influence of the Manicheans but wanted to live a good life. However, he was too weak to change, even though at his mother's insistence he sent his mistress back to Africa. Soon after, he had taken another woman into his house.

In Milan he came to know the Neo-Platonists and came under the influence of St. Ambrose, who was the bishop of Milan. He learned authentic Catholic teaching and then went through a crisis which he describes in *The Confessions*. He converted, resigned his teaching position and in 387 was baptized by St. Ambrose. He formed a community with his followers, mother and son, and then he prepared to return to Africa. His mother died on the way. He returned to Tagaste in 388 and established a religious community. Adeodatus, his son of 15 years, died the next year.

Augustine went to Hippo in 391, where he was ordained a priest and made an administrator. He was consecrated bishop of Hippo in 395. He spent 40 years as a priest and bishop. Through his preaching and writing, he fought the Manicheans, Donatists (violent schismatics resentful of Roman influence in their religion and life) and Pelagians (who denied original sin and the need of grace for salvation). After Alaric led the barbarians to capture Rome, Augustine wrote *The City of God*, beginning that monumental work in 413 and completing it in 426. That work described the city of man and the city of God, and in it he also discussed the many heresies which were popular at the time.

In 430 the Vandals laid siege to Hippo. Augustine became ill and died on August 26, 430.

Unit 4: Philosophy ~ Religion

Books I-X of The Confessions

by St. Augustine of Hippo
Translation: Henry Chadwick
Oxford World's Classics

The Confessions is a statement of what Augustine had done during his life and what he had now become, directed to God. It is not only a confession of sins but also of temptations and an acknowledgment of God's grace by which he was saved. True to the meaning of the word *confession*, this is a three-fold confession of sins, of faith, and of praise to God.

In the midst of his degradation, Augustine had a sense that the way he was living his life was wrong, and he had a desire to rise above his error. The struggle out of his degradation was, however, a difficult and long road. He persisted, and not only did he rise above his sins of the flesh, but his will and intellect were also converted.

The Confessions has three distinct divisions. Books I-IX are the story of Augustine's life from birth to his conversion and his mother's death. They cover 33 years. Book X describes his state of mind, and is an examination of conscience about present problems. Books XI-XIII are a study of Genesis and a meditation on eternity.

The book is written as a prolonged meditation. It is a prayer addressed to God, characterized by vivid imagery, narrative and character studies. Even though *The Confessions* is addressed to God, Augustine's work speaks to every human heart.

This study guide covers the first 10 books of *The Confessions*.

Unit 4: Philosophy ~ Religion

Book I

1. How does St. Augustine begin *The Confessions*?
2. What are some of Augustine's questions of God?
3. What is God?
4. What does he want God to say to him?
5. Augustine acknowledges that the source even of the milk he drank as an infant was what?
6. Does he remember his infancy?
7. What question does Augustine ask of God regarding the time before his birth?
8. What does he say about an infant's will?
9. When did he first encounter great misery?
10. How did he sin as a student?
11. How does he contrast the behavior of adults and children?
12. What motivated Augustine in his disobedience?
13. Did Augustine believe in God at this time?
14. Was he baptized as a youngster?
15. What does he say about the fact that he was forced to study and learn?
16. What did Augustine like to study?
17. What did he weep over?
18. How did Augustine learn Latin and Greek?
19. Why did Homer give divine attributes to vicious men (gods)?
20. As a youth, how did Augustine respond to the filth that was taught him?

21. In addition to learning and delighting in the filth of the stage, what other debaucheries did Augustine fall into?

22. Were these just childish acts?

Book II

1. What does Augustine say his parents were most concerned about?

2. At what age were his studies in Madauros interrupted, allowing him to spend time in idleness?

3. What does he say about his mother at this time?

4. Was God silent at this time?

5. What was most important to Augustine during this time?

6. Why did his parents desire his education and not "burden" him with a wife?

7. What did Augustine steal?

8. Why did he do it?

9. Why, according to Augustine, do men sin?

10. Augustine thanks God for all he has been given, and for what else?

Book III

1. What does Augustine attribute his lust to?

2. What irony does he speak about regarding the theater?

3. What did he study in Carthage?

4. What does Augustine say about Cicero's work?

5. What influence did Cicero's work have on Augustine?

6. What did the work of Cicero lack?

Unit 4: Philosophy ~ Religion

7. What did Augustine pursue?

8. Why did the Scriptures fail to "speak" to Augustine?

9. To whom was he attracted as a result?

10. What superstition did the Manicheans have about food?

11. What was Monica's dream?

12. How did Augustine interpret the dream?

13. What purpose did the dream serve?

14. Why did the bishop Ambrose refuse to talk to Augustine as Monica requested?

15. What did the bishop predict?

16. What final words did the bishop have for Monica?

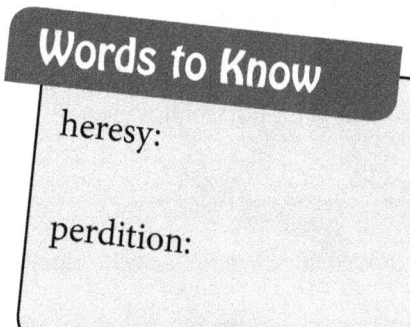

Words to Know

heresy:

perdition:

Book IV

1. What practice of the soothsayers did Augustine abhor?

2. Whom did he consult?

3. Why was Augustine overcome with sadness?

4. Why did Augustine leave Tagaste?

5. On what did Augustine base his love for Hierius?

6. What did Augustine desire for himself?

7. What gifts did Augustine have?

Book V

1. Why was Augustine disappointed when he finally met Faustus, the "great teacher?"

2. As a result, what happened to Augustine?

The Confessions

3. Why did Augustine want to go to Rome?

4. How did Augustine deceive his mother?

5. What did Augustine do in Rome?

6. How did he happen to go to Milan?

7. Who was in Milan who would greatly influence him?

8. What was Augustine's interest at the time?

Book VI

1. What was the cause of Augustine's depression?

2. What did Monica do, which was forbidden by Bishop Ambrose?

3. Why did Ambrose forbid this?

4. Did Augustine have personal or intimate contact with Ambrose? Why?

5. What did Augustine say about the Scriptures?

6. How would you contrast Augustine and the drunk beggar?

7. What was the lesson of Alypius and the circus?

8. Who arranged Augustine's marriage?

9. What did Augustine and his friends desire?

10. What happened to Augustine's mistress?

11. What did Augustine dread as punishment for his sins?

Question for Further Thought

What was the philosophy of Epicurus?

Book VII

1. How did Augustine perceive God to be at this time?

2. What is the Christian explanation of evil?

3. What did Augustine spend much time trying to discover?

4. What example did he give of the fates of two people with the same horoscope?

5. What did this prove about horoscopes?

6. In his search for the truth, what was one way Augustine conceived of Christ?

7. What books of Scripture did Augustine begin to read first?

Book VIII

1. Who was Simplicianus?

2. What did Simplicianus say about the writings of the Platonists?

3. Who was Victorinus?

4. What two wills in Augustine were in conflict?

5. Why could Augustine no longer use the excuse of ignorance?

6. When Augustine was in the final stages in his struggle for continence, why did he separate himself from his friend Alypius?

7. While he was weeping, what did he hear?

8. What did he do?

9. What specifically did he read?

10. What did it say?

11. After telling Alypius, what did Augustine do?

Book IX

1. What did Augustine resolve to do?
2. What did he mean "to give in my name?"
3. Who else was baptized with Augustine?
4. What became of Adeodatus?
5. Why were hymns and canticles sung?
6. How did Monica's maidservant teach her moderation?
7. Nevertheless, what did Monica do?
8. Why did she stop?
9. What policy of behavior did Monica have toward her husband?
10. What other gift did Monica have?
11. What changed in Patrick once he converted?
12. What did Monica tell Augustine at Ostia about what she had wanted in life?
13. What was Monica's attitude about where she was to be buried?

Book X

1. What answer did Augustine understand when he asked God, "who are you?"
2. What does Augustine say about memory?
3. Besides images, what else does the memory encompass?
4. What does Augustine ask about the things learned and stored in the memory?
5. What is the meaning of cogitation as understood by Augustine?
6. What else does memory contain?
7. Is God to be found in the memory?

Unit 4: Philosophy ~ Religion

8. What does Augustine say is necessary to desire in order to have happiness?

9. What is his question with regard to happiness?

10. What is the only happiness?

11. Since Augustine learned about God, where has God resided?

12. What daily pleasure does Augustine try to suppress?

13. With regard to music, when does Augustine say he sins?

14. What is lust of the eyes?

15. What dilemma does Augustine have regarding praise?

16. What temptation do people fall into regarding being pleased with themselves?

17. In summary, what are the three forms of lust that Augustine has considered?

18. The wages of sin is death; what are the wages of righteousness?

Words to Know

Manichaeism:

Donatism:

concupiscence:

Research Topic:

Research the different heresies which arose in the early Church. Who were their teachers, what did they teach and how did the Church respond? How has the heresy of Gnosticism reappeared today, and what has been its impact?

A beautiful passage in *The Confessions* is to be found in Section 38 of Book X, beginning with "Late have I loved you." This summarizes the theme of this wonderful work. Memorize this section through "You touched me, and I am set on fire to attain the peace which is yours."

Books I-X of The City of God

by St. Augustine of Hippo
Translation: Henry Bettenson
Penguin Classics

The City of God is St. Augustine's meditation on the decline of the Roman Empire. Rome had ruled supreme for 1000 years when it was sacked. He began to write it three years after Rome was sacked by the Goths under Alaric in 410 A.D.

The book took 13 years to write. In the first 10 books, St. Augustine wrote about Christianity versus paganism; in the second half of this huge work he moved on to the theology of two cities: the earthly city and the heavenly city, and to God's intervention in human history.

In brief, the theology of St. Augustine emphasizes:
- the idea that life is lived according to one's beliefs
- that Christianity is the life, death and resurrection of Christ in the hearts and souls of individuals and society
- that those who live in the City of God are united by the love of God and of one another (charity)
- that those who live in the other city are not united: they oppose God and they love themselves first (cupidity)

The two cities can and do coexist. St. Augustine asserts that "all the good and evil of history, all the prosperity and adversity which come upon the saints in this life serve only to forward the growth of the Mystical Christ." The Mystical Christ is the communion of the faithful with Christ, formed through the Church into a single body with Christ as the head.

Unit 4: Philosophy ~ Religion

Book I

1. What places were untouched during the sack of Rome?
2. Who took refuge in the churches?
3. Why do the righteous also suffer?
4. What does St. Augustine say about the pagan gods?
5. During the war, what happened in the pagan temples?
6. The calamities which Rome experienced were the result of what customs?
7. What does God will for both good and evil people?
8. Then what is the difference between the fates of good and evil people?
9. What fault do the good fall into?
10. Why are good people seemingly punished equally with the bad?
11. What does St. Augustine say about the end of life?
12. Does lack of burial hinder resurrection?
13. Why should the bodies of the dead be buried?
14. What lessons did Marcus Regulus teach?
15. What is the lesson of Regulus?
16. What does Augustine say about suicide?
17. Does a woman sin who is violated by another without her consent?
18. Why did Lucretia bear the heavier punishment?
19. When may one be justified in killing another?
20. When may a suicide be allowed?

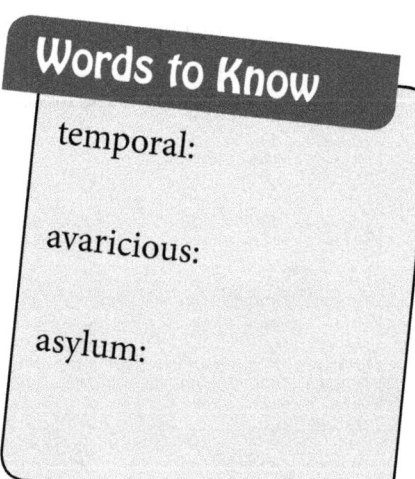

Words to Know

temporal:

avaricious:

asylum:

The City of God

21. Why does God allow the pure to be violated?

22. Why do the Romans complain about Christianity?

23. What had Scipio Nasica feared for Rome?

24. To what do avarice and luxury lead?

25. Public games were established by what?

26. What had Scipio prohibited?

27. To what does St. Augustine attribute the fact that so many Romans are still alive?

28. What had Romulus and Remus done to increase the population of the city they founded?

29. What does St. Augustine say of the two cities (the heavenly city and the earthly one)?

Book II

1. Instead of blaming the sack of Rome on the Christians, what should the pagans be doing?

2. How had Rome been destroyed before the wall fell?

3. What had the pagan gods failed to do?

4. What does St. Augustine say about the religious rites performed for the pagan gods?

5. What other virtues had the gods failed to teach?

6. To whom do the philosophers belong?

7. Why can't we rely on the philosophers for moral training?

8. What question does St. Augustine raise about the philosophers?

9. Why had dramatic entertainments been started in Rome?

10. Why did the Greeks honor their poets and actors?

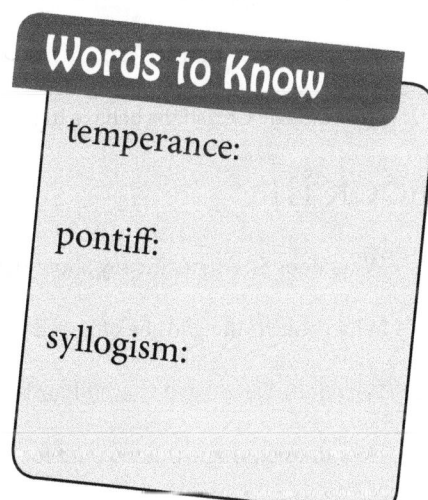

Words to Know

temperance:

pontiff:

syllogism:

Unit 4: Philosophy ~ Religion

11. How were the Romans different?

12. What does St. Augustine say about the Roman gods?

13. What, then, is the inconsistency?

14. What syllogism does St. Augustine give us in this regard?

15. What did Plato say about poets?

16. What were the statutes of Roman law called?

17. During what brief period did Rome become great and "justice and morality prevailed among them by nature as much as by law?" (Sallust)

18. Sallust further identified the real cause of civility and good order. What was it?

19. What are the dominant concerns of the Romans?

20. How had Scipio defined a republic?

21. The gods of the Romans lent divine authority to what?

22. How did the Christians behave in contrast to the Romans?

Book III

1. What does St. Augustine say about perjury?

2. Why couldn't the gods be offended by Paris' adultery?

3. Why does Varro say it is useful for brave men to believe they are descended from the gods?

4. How does St. Augustine account for the gods leaving Troy and coming to Rome?

5. What crime did the gods seem to tolerate?

6. Why does St. Augustine not attribute Numa's peace to the gods?

7. What did the Romans feel compelled to do as the empire grew?

Words to Know

mountebank:

sacrilege:

propitiate:

8. What does St. Augustine attribute the war with Alba to?

9. What does St. Augustine say about the deaths of the kings?

10. In the period "when the commonwealth was governed with equity, justice and moderation came to an end" what was the general situation in Rome?

11. What put an end to the strife?

12. Why was the Battle of Cannae notable?

13. What was the saddest disaster of the Second Punic War? Why?

14. What does this say about the gods?

15. What do the stories of Regulus and Saguntum have in common?

16. Sallust says that which period was the time of the greatest virtue among Romans?

17. What are some things that were introduced from Asia into Rome?

18. What reward did Scipio receive from the gods and indeed from Rome for his victory over Hannibal?

19. What was the *Lex Vaconia*?

20. What was St. Augustine's opinion of the *Lex Vaconia*?

21. To what was the Temple of Concord a memorial?

22. Was the temple effective against sedition?

23. Who was the avenger of the cruelties of Marius?

24. St. Augustine says that during Sylla's time peace competed with war in cruelty and surpassed it. Why?

25. What had Rome's own historians said about her civil wars?

26. Before what great event did these and many other wars take place?

27. What is the irony about which St. Augustine writes?

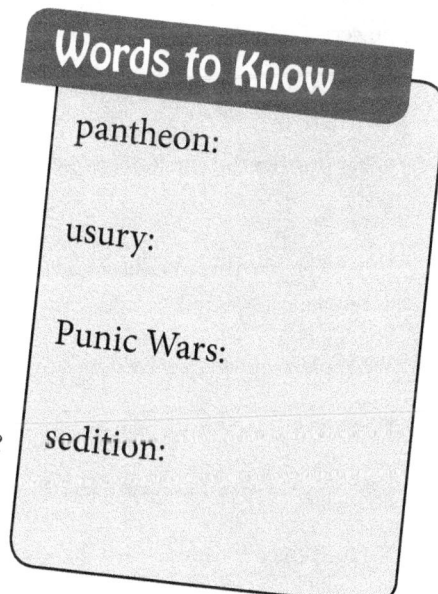

Words to Know

pantheon:

usury:

Punic Wars:

sedition:

Unit 4: Philosophy ~ Religion

Book IV

1. What question does St. Augustine pose at the beginning of Chapter 3 regarding the Roman Empire?

2. What does St. Augustine say about the evils imposed on the just by the unjust?

3. When Rome was enjoying control over so many subjects and had conquered so many foreign lands, she still was fearful of people who were not loyal. What group proved to be a great threat to her from 73-71 B.C.?

4. By naming the many gods who are in charge of so many diverse things, what is St. Augustine trying to show?

5. What would happen if only Jupiter were worshipped?

6. Why can it not be that God is the soul and the world His body?

7. What do Plato and other philosophers say of the gods?

8. According to St. Augustine, what are felicity and virtue?

9. Of the Roman gods, which one does St. Augustine say should have been worshipped because of her powers? Why?

10. Why is Felicity not a goddess?

11. What practice did the Romans follow in the naming of gods?

12. What were the three kinds of gods distinguished by Scaevola?

13. What place did augury hold in Rome?

14. What did Cicero think of auguries?

15. Why did Varro not publish everything "known about the gods?"

16. Varro seemed to lean toward the worship of what?

17. According to Varro, how could the rites of religion have been more purely observed?

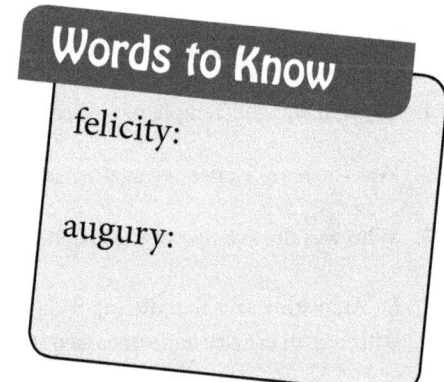

Words to Know

felicity:

augury:

18. To whom does God give felicity?

19. From whom do earthly kingdoms come?

20. What does St. Augustine say of the Jews?

Book V

1. How did many people during this period understand destiny?

2. Can destiny be separate from the will of God?

3. What was Hippocrates' understanding of the case of the two brothers who became ill at the same time, whose illness followed the same course and who returned to health at the same time?

4. What was the Stoic Posidonius' understanding of the same course of events?

5. How can we know that the position of the stars does not determine our future?

6. What was a second understanding of fate or destiny?

7. What does St. Augustine call this understanding of "fate?"

8. What did Cicero believe about fate?

9. What is the conflict with the belief in foreknowledge?

10. Why can we not deny that God has foreknowledge of future events?

11. What did Cicero fear about the belief in God's foreknowledge of future things?

12. How does St. Augustine state Christian belief?

13. How can we account for our wills?

14. Why are wicked wills not from the Creator?

15. The Cause of things, which makes but is not made, is what?

16. What are subordinated to this Cause?

17. Why is God said to be all-powerful?

Unit 4: Philosophy ~ Religion

18. To what should we attribute suffering contrary to our own will?

19. How did Sallust describe the ancient Romans?

20. Of whom did Sallust say the "the less he sought glory the more it pursued him?"

21. To what did Cato attribute the rewards of virtue in his day?

22. What was he lamenting?

23. To what did Cato attribute the successes of the empire after the kings were removed?

24. What reward did they receive who sought glory?

25. What reward will the saints (Christians) receive who endure much in the earthly city and remain faithful?

26. What two things does St. Augustine say compelled the Romans to do admirable deeds?

27. Who gave power to all the emperors, Roman and foreign, throughout history?

28. What did the defeat of Radagaisus show the Romans?

29. What was the happiness of the Christian emperors?

30. In conclusion, what does St. Augustine say about God's gifts?

Words to Know

destiny:

prescience:

omnipotent:

inscrutable:

prodigal:

QUESTIONS FOR FURTHER THOUGHT

A. Do Christians believe in fate?

B. What do Christians believe about the causes of events in their lives?

Book VI

1. What was Cicero's opinion of Varro?

2. Who was Varro?

3. Varro divided theology into three kinds. What were they?

4. What did the Mythical theology contain?

5. What did he say about Physical (natural) theology?

6. What did he say about Civil theology?

7. What was Seneca's opinion of the Jews?

Book VII

1. What "advantage" did the inferior gods have over the select deities?

2. Why did Jupiter have so many titles?

3. How does Augustine account for the various stories of the pagan gods?

4. How does the God of the Christians differ from the pagan gods?

5. Why were Numa's books burned?

Words to Know

elucidation:

omnipotent:

Question for Further Thought

We have seen that Jupiter had many titles. Christians follow a similar practice in attributing more than one title to Christ. What are some of the titles they address Him by?

Unit 4: Philosophy ~ Religion

Book VIII

1. With whom must we confer in discussing natural theology?
2. What do philosophers whom St. Augustine seeks to refute believe?
3. What were the two schools of philosophy?
4. Who founded the Italic school and where was it?
5. What had philosophers been called before Pythagoras coined the name?
6. Who founded the Ionic school?
7. Who directed the effort of philosophy to the correction and regulation of morality?
8. What had been the focus of previous philosophers?
9. Why did Socrates strive for a pure life?
10. What is the *summum bonum*?
11. What two things does the study of wisdom consist of?
12. Who combined the two?
13. How did Plato divide philosophy?
14. What is another name for logic?
15. What did Plato determine to be the final good?
16. What did Plato see as the highest good?
17. How would Plato define a philosopher?
18. On what main point did the Platonists and the Christians disagree?
19. What did Plato believe about the gods?
20. What is the three-fold division of rational souls, according to the Platonists?

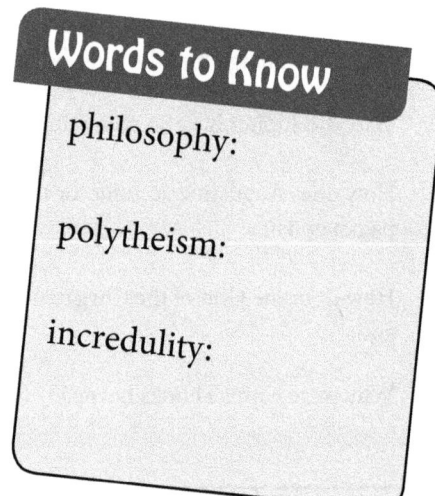

Words to Know

philosophy:

polytheism:

incredulity:

21. How does St. Augustine describe the demons?

22. According to Apuleius, what function did the demons have?

23. What do Christians believe about demons?

24. What was Hermes' belief?

25. What did Hermes appear to predict?

26. What conflict do we see in Hermes' thought?

27. How do we resemble the good angels?

28. How are we different from the good angels?

29. Why do we honor the martyrs?

Question for Further Thought

How is the honor given the martyrs and saints different from the worship of God?

Book IX

1. How have people settled the problem of "bad gods?"

2. Why are demons miserable?

3. How does this separate them from the gods?

4. How do wise men control their passions and affections?

5. What do the passions which Christians feel do for them?

6. In his description of the demons, what did Apuleius fail to do?

7. Why, according to Plotinus, would demons be more wretched than men?

Unit 4: Philosophy ~ Religion

8. What function did the Platonists believe the demons served?

9. What were the gods to have that man did not?

10. Who is the only possible mediator between God and men? Why?

11. What is the true nature of demons?

12. What is the origin of the word demon?

13. What is the problem with the knowledge of the demons?

14. How does the knowledge of the angels differ from that of the demons?

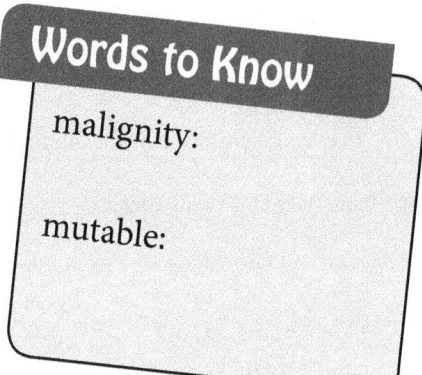

Words to Know

malignity:

mutable:

Book X

1. Why does St. Augustine say the Platonists are the best known philosophers?

2. Where is the error of the Platonists?

3. What words does St. Augustine discuss which have to do with the worship of God and which can be misunderstood if not used carefully?

4. What did visible sacrifices signify?

5. What is the purpose of sacrifice?

6. How can good angels be distinguished from bad angels?

7. Who aided tyrants in their hatred of the City of God?

8. Why were they given power to harm Christians?

9. What is the universal way for the soul's liberation?

10. St. Augustine concludes Book X with a summary. What has he done in the first five books?

11. What has he done in the second set of five books?

Questions for Further Thought

A. What was the basic format of St. Augustine's work? Was it effective?

B. Why should we read about pagan thought?

Sources Consulted

Augustine, St. 2003. *City of God*, trans. Henry Bettenson. New York. Penguin Books.

Augustine, St. 2009. *The Confession of St. Augustine*, trans. Henry Chadwick. Oxford. Oxford World Classics.

Aurelius, Marcus. 1964. *Meditations*, trans. Maxwell Staniforth. New York. Penguin Books.

Cicero. 1971. *Selected Works*, trans. Michael Grant. New York. Penguin Books.

Cowan, Louise and Os Guinness. 1998. *Invitation to the Classics*. Grand Rapids. Baker Books.

Duckworth, George E. 1967. *The Complete Roman Drama*. New York. Random House.

Graves, Robert, ed. 1962. *The Comedies of Terence*. Chicago. Aldine Publishing Company.

Hadas, Moses, and the Editors of Time-Life Books. 1965. *Imperial Rome*. New York. Time-Life Books.

Hamilton, Edith. 1963. *The Roman Way*. New York. New American Library (A Mentor Book).

Harvey, Sir Paul. 1962. *The Oxford Companion to Classical Literature*. Oxford. Oxford University Press.

Livy. 1971. *The Early History of Rome*, trans. Aubrey de Selincourt. New York. Penguin Books.

Livy. 1972. *The War with Hannibal*, trans. Aubrey de Selincourt. New York. Penguin Books.

Ovid. 1958. *The Metamorphoses*, trans. Horace Gregory. New York. New American Library (A Mentor Book).

Plautus. 1965. *The Pot of Gold and Other Plays*, trans. E.F. Watling. New York. Penguin Books.

Sallust. 1963. *The Jugurthine War/The Conspiracy of Catiline*. New York. Penguin Books.

Snodgrass, Mary Ellen. M.A. 1988. *Cliff Notes on Roman Classics*. Lincoln. Cliff Notes.

Tacitus. 1996. *The Annals of Imperial Rome*, trans. Michael Grant. New York. Penguin Books.

Sources

Staniforth, Maxwell, trans. 1968. *Early Christian Writings / The Apostolic Fathers,*. Baltimore. Penguin Books.

Virgil. 1990. *The Aeneid*, trans. Robert Fitzgerald. New York. Vintage Classics.

Wikipedia.org   Topic - Roman Numerals

Wilson-Okamura, David, trans. 2005. http://virgil.org/vitae/

About the Author

Fran Rutherford was the primary educator of her children for 16 years, during which time she taught the Classics using a couple of the programs available to homeschool parents. When she began, the curricula available did not flesh out the readings or provide an analysis of the works studied. Deciding to read the books before the children, Fran began to write questions which would help the children to focus on the main ideas put forth, and the result is three study guides, covering the readings of most classical curricula for high school students.

Those study guides are now available in both Student Guides and Teacher Guides. They are: *Greek Classics*, *Ancient Rome*, and *Old World Europe*. They have proven to be very helpful for both students and their teachers in understanding the works which form the foundation of Western Civilization.

Fran has been a speaker at various homeschooling conferences and gatherings and encourages parents to educate their children through the high school years. She is available to speak on topics relating to classical curricula, as well as the "how-to" of actually doing it. Her latest talk "Beauty and the Beast" explored the notion of beauty and how the classics help incorporate it into our lives.

Fran can be reached through her blog or at Classicstudyguides.com with any questions relative to Questions for the Thinker Study Guides© or Questions for the Thinker Ebook Study Guides©, as well as to schedule talks.

About the Illustrator

James Rutherford was born in Albuquerque, New Mexico, the third child of Larry and Fran Rutherford. He showed an extraordinary aptitude for music and drawing at a young age. After completing the fifth grade, his parents decided to educate him at home and afford him the time to not only get a rigorous education, but also to have the time to spend on his music and art. He studied the Classics of Greece and Rome, Europe and America when he was in high school and accompanied his assignments with beautiful illustrations of the gods and other subjects of interest.

James attended the University of Dallas, graduating *cum laude* with a Bachelor's Degree in Art and Sculpture. He went on to receive his Master's degree in Web Design and New Media from Academy of Art University graduating *magna cum laude*. He currently lives in Monument, CO with his beautiful wife and two daughters.

www.ingramcontent.com/pod-product-compliance
Lightning Source LLC
Chambersburg PA
CBHW081132170426
43197CB00017B/2837